YOUR HOME DOCTOR™
Babies

Dr. Robert Fallis

THE MEDIUS PUBLISHING GROUP

USA • CANADA

Your Home Doctor™ - Babies
Copyright ® 1997, 1999 Dr. Robert Fallis

Canadian Cataloguing in Publication Data

Fallis, Robert
   Babies

(Your Home Doctor™)
ISBN 1-894434-00-5

1. Infants–Health and hygiene. 2. Pediatrics–Popular works. I. Title II. Series

RJ61.F34 1999   618.92   C99-931619-2

Book Design & Layout: Gordon Bate
Author Photograph: Michelle Newberry

Printed in Canada

Published by The Medius Publishing Group,
a division of Your Home Doctor™ Inc.,
Suite 204 - 245 Pelham Road, St. Catharines, Ontario L2S 1X8
Web: http://www.yourhomedoctor.com

pgs. 120 - 125 Reproduced with permission
Copyright Infant / Child Performance Guidelines for CPR, 1994,
Heart and Stroke Foundation of Canada

This book is dedicated to
my patients and family.
To my patients who have taught me
the joy and humility of being a family doctor.
To my parents who have taught me
about love, responsibility and sacrifice.
To Cathy who has taught me
about balance and perspective.
To Kim, Andrew, Shari and Brian who have taught me
about the incredible strength of family.
To Kelsey, Trent, Alanna, Tyler, Paige and Kerry who
continue to teach me the value of a child's perspective on life
encompassing honesty, innocence, enthusiasm, curiosity,
and boundless energy.
What better way to explore and experience the
beauty and wonder of the world in which we live.

Foreword

One of the most frightening experiences in life is becoming a parent for the first time. Even the best prepared parents are shocked to find how insecure and uncertain their new baby makes them feel. This book is written with the average scared parent in mind.

The author systematically reviews all the common health problems of infants and young children. The presentation is attractive, concise and the flow charts are easy to follow.

Dr. Fallis quite correctly encourages parents to trust their instincts and have their child checked by a doctor if they truly believe something is wrong. This book will be a very welcome addition to any young family's home library. It should reassure new parents and help them to make correct decisions about their child's health care needs.

Above all, this book is written in a casual style with ample use of humour. The last section is full of tips and suggestions which should be reviewed not only by parents but by grandparents and all adults who occasionally have "little people" in their homes. Let us all do our best to make our children's living space safe and secure.

D.A. Jarvis, M.D., F.R.C.P.C
Director of Emergency Services
Department of Pediatrics
The Hospital for Sick Children
Toronto, Ontario

Acknowledgements

I would like to thank all those that have reviewed the
book and provided support for this project.
Their assistance and guidance has been invaluable.

Physician/Pharmacist Resource Team

Paul Faulkner, MD, CCFP(EM)
Shari Fallis, MD, CCFP
Nancy Fung,MD, CCFP
Sylvia Fung, Bpharm
D.A. Jarvis, MB,BS,FRCPC,FAAP
Michael Kopp, MD, CCFP(EM)
John McCauley, MD, CCFP
Christina Plaskos, MD
Ivan Samson, MD,FRCPC
John Schultz, MD, CCFP
Ashok Sharma, MD, CCFPC
Kevin Smith, MD,FRCPC
Lain Venditelli, BEd, DDS

Nurse, Breast Feeding and Parent Resource Team

Jennifer Boise, RN
Briar Campbell, RN
Susan Dolan, RN
Kim Howell, BEd, LLB
Marion Lips-Smith, BA
Julie Montpelier, RN
Toni Samson

A very special thanks to Paul Heron and Gordon Bate
for their very rare blend of organizational skills
with creative panache.

To Brian Vandenberg who, with unwavering dedication,
made it all possible. Thanks Buddy.

Introduction

Kids Get Sick with Surprising Regularity

As a father of three as well as a family and emergency physician, I am well aware of the 3 am medical crisis. Erma Bombeck once commented that "children only seem to get sick after hours and on weekends when the rates go up." Regardless of their motives, the reality is that children get sick with surprising regularity. The fact is that it is well within the normal range for otherwise healthy preschool children to acquire anywhere from six to 12 infections per year. With these kinds of odds it only makes sense to get ready for the onslaught once you start having children.

Parent Support Structures Missing

There is nothing more frightening than being up in the middle of the night with a sick child and not knowing what to do. I have unfortunately found, through my years of practice, that often the normal support facilities for new parents, including grandparents, uncles, aunts, etc., are no longer readily accessible to the learning parent. The reality of the modern day is that the family support for new parents may live several thousands of miles away. Therefore, new moms and dads often rely heavily on books, friends and their family doctor to advise them on general infant care and treatment.

The Parent Learning Curve Is Immense

In writing this book I have attempted to put on paper (actually computer hard disc) what I have learned over time from hundreds of parents and grandparents. By tempering this with medical insight, my hope was to provide an easy to follow, systematic approach to infant care that could be followed even in the middle of the night. This is the same approach I use for parents in both my office and the emergency room. By concentrating on practical treatments, tips and trade secrets, my wish is to provide treatment options and relief to both suffering parties, child and parent.

Getting Back to the Basics

With the vast amount of information and treatment choices available to today's parents, I wanted to help parents get "back to the basics" by providing them with the essentials needed to help them treat their sick child with comfort and security.

Your Home Doctor™ *Babies* is not meant to be a textbook on pediatric health. This book is meant to be "meat and potato's " medicine. It deals with 25 of the most common medical conditions that you are likely to encounter in the first two years of your baby's life. It is meant as a bridge to help get you through the night and on to your family doctor the next day. Alternatively, it tells you when as a parent you should abandon home treatment and seek emergency medical services (EMS). For most people this means an ambulance or the local emergency department.

Parents' Intuition

Foremost I want to encourage parents to trust their instincts. Parents' intuition is the innate sixth sense that parents develop soon after the birth of their child. Parents often instinctively know when things are not right with their baby. If you become uncomfortable, if you start to feel the hairs on your neck stand up when caring for your sick baby, that's parents' intuition. Listen to it! Have your child checked by a doctor.

Awareness and Preparedness

I have long since discovered that the difference between good parents and great parents all comes down to awareness and preparedness. To be aware of potential problems is one thing. To be prepared for this possibility by either attempting to prevent the occurrence or preparing for treatment of the unpreventible (e.g., the common cold) is the second. It is for this reason that the Boy Scouts' motto "be prepared" should be the motto of all parents.

Becoming a Proactive Parent

In purchasing this book you have taken the initiative. A proactive approach is imperative. Trust your instincts and become aware and prepared. My sincere wish is that this book may provide you with a measure of relief, reassurance and sleep – and make your parenting adventure at least a little easier.

Sincerely,

Dr. Robert Fallis

Humour... Your Beacon in the Storm

Humour and quotations are sprinkled throughout the book. As a parent, up at 3 in the morning with a sick child on one shoulder and vomit on the other, what else is there but humour to help get you through?

A note of explanation: Throughout the book I often suggest that parents should take their child to their family doctor. For every family, this family doctor may be different. For many it will be a certified family physician or general practitioner, for others it will be a pediatrician or general internist. Your family physician is whomever you trust to look after the best interests of your baby and family.

Please make use of the variety of information available in this book (i.e., case studies, symptoms, tips, warnings, flow charts, definitions) to better facilitate the care of your child. Remember that children with other health problems often need to be seen by a doctor sooner than described in this book.

I love to hear from parents – you are the experts in the evolving art of caring for sick children. Your comments, questions or funny anecdotes are always welcome.

How to Use This Book

This book has been written with the goal that it will be the first book you pick up when your baby is ill or injured. In an age when you can download the entire archives of a medical library to your home computer, we are in desperate need of getting back to the basics. That is, knowing what is most important, or getting "Just the facts, ma'am."

What I have attempted to do in Your Home Doctor™ Babies is deal with the 25 most common medical conditions that affect children aged 0 – 2 years. This book is in no way intended to be a textbook on any of the subjects. Rather, this should be a first-approach book when dealing with these common medical concerns of babies.

To assist the care giver, I have tried to group the most important information on any given topic within the four pages written on each condition. The information is presented in several formats to assist you in connecting to the book in some meaningful way.

For those who can best identify with examples, I have written case studies for each of the medical conditions. They are written using the most common symptoms, age, sex and scenarios to make them real for you.

For those who learn best with conventional medical information styles, you will find the warning, symptoms, and tip page most helpful.

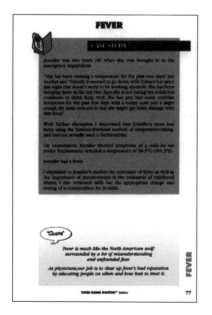

Become "one" with this book

I thoroughly endorse the idea of making books interactive. This means it's okay to write, doodle or jot down notes, thoughts or other concerns in this book. Make this book part of your life. The more functional a book becomes, the more useful it is. I give you my full permission to write away (I won't even tell your parents or old school teacher).

Be sure to always read the warnings prior to treating your child. Remember, if you are at all in doubt, or your parental intuition is kicking in, have your baby checked immediately by your family doctor or at the emergency department.

By including 'Trade Secrets', 'Medications/Treatments', 'Definitions' and 'Synonyms', the hope is to provide you with all that you require on each topic at a flip of a page. Synonyms are included because I have found over the years that parents don't often understand the jargon used in the medical profession to explain treatment and diseases. Providing popular words for some of this jargon should help to demystify the process of treating sick kids.

Those who deal best with information in a visual format will find the flow charts the easiest approach when diagnosing and treating an ill baby.

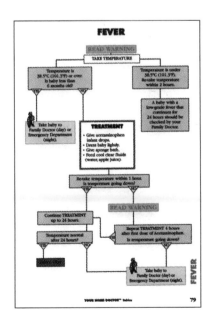

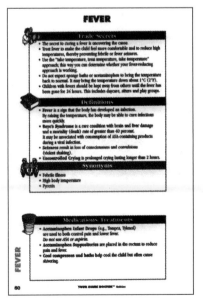

CONTENTS

Table of Contents

CONTENTS continued

Table of Contents

CASE STUDY

Martin was 22 months old when he was brought in to the emergency department. His mother was frantic.

"He just developed a rash all over his body within the past hour," she exclaimed. "Now he is getting some swelling around his eyes and just started scratching all over."

Examination revealed an uncomfortable boy with watery eyes and a runny nose. He had swelling around his face and eyes and had developed hives over the rest of his body. He was not having difficulty breathing but looked miserable. Further information from his mother indicated that he had been on antibiotics for five days for an ear infection. One hour prior to developing the rash, Martin had eaten a peanut butter and jelly sandwich and drank a glass of strawberry fruit punch.

Martin was having an allergic reaction.

Allergic reactions are like a flat tire on your car: they can happen to anyone at any time and any place.

ALLERGIC REACTIONS

SYMPTOMS

- Sneezing • Stuffed-up or runny nose • Itchy or watery eyes
- Swelling of lips, eyelids or skin • Skin rash (hives) or itching
- Wheezing, coughing or difficulty breathing or swallowing

GOALS

Treat symptoms. Determine what caused the allergic reaction.

TIPS

- Always remove the cause if possible (for example, the bee stinger).
- Antihistamines help treat the reaction.
- Decongestants may relieve congestion, watery eyes and sneezing.
- Allergic reactions are an overreaction to something baby has had to eat or drink, or has inhaled, touched or has injected.
- Allergies are not from something new.
  They are reactions to something baby has been exposed to before.
- Asthma and eczema may also be caused by allergies.
- Food allergies are over-diagnosed. Only 5 to 10 percent of children have true food allergies. Most common food allergies are to peanuts, egg whites, berries, seafood or dairy products.
- For itching, try colloidal or oatmeal baths or calamine lotion.
  Persistent itching may require an antihistamine, available from your pharmacist or by prescription from your family doctor.
- Do not smoke around children or in their homes.
- Get a Medic-Alert bracelet for your child with severe allergic reactions.
- Get an anaphylaxis kit (ana-kit) for your child with severe allergic reactions.

ALLERGIC REACTIONS

ALLERGIC REACTIONS

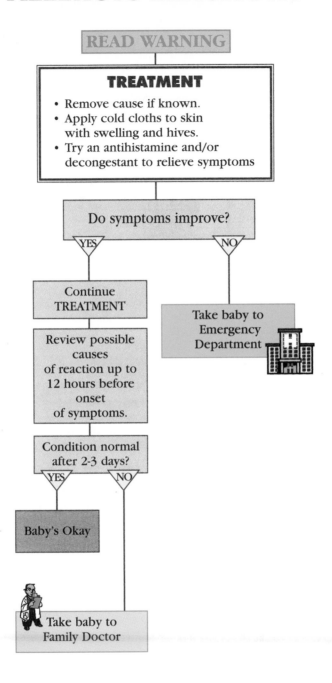

READ WARNING

TREATMENT

- Remove cause if known.
- Apply cold cloths to skin with swelling and hives.
- Try an antihistamine and/or decongestant to relieve symptoms

Do symptoms improve?

YES

NO

Continue
TREATMENT

Take baby to
Emergency
Department

Review possible
causes
of reaction up to
12 hours before
onset
of symptoms.

Condition normal
after 2-3 days?

YES

NO

Baby's Okay

Take baby to
Family Doctor

ALLERGIC REACTIONS

Trade Secrets

- The treatment of allergic reactions depends on severity of the symptoms.
- Some of the most common causes of allergic reactions include cigarette smoke, nuts, seafood, antibiotics, milk, eggs, citrus juice, pollens and plants, insect bites and stings, and latex products.
- Symptoms of allergic reactions can recur for up to 72 hours after exposure to the cause.

Definitions

- **Allergic reactions** are an overreaction of the body's immune system to a foreign substance (usually one that it has been exposed to before).
- **Asthma** is a lung condition of troubled breathing and wheezing.
- **Eczema** is an inflammatory skin rash with itching and weeping.
- **Hives** are itchy, red bumps on the skin that may occur with allergic reactions.
- **Inhaled** means to breathe in.
- **Injected** means to have a needle.
- **Wheezing** is a musical, whistling sound heard when breathing tubes are restricted. Wheezing is usually heard when breathing out.

Synonyms

- Anaphylaxis
- Anaphylactoid reaction

Medications/Treatments

- **Adrenaline** (e.g., epinephrine, Epi-Pen) is an injected medicine used in bee-sting kits, ana-kits and emergency departments to treat severe allergic reactions.
- **Antihistamines** (e.g., Benadryl, Atarax, Claritin) are used to reduce the histamine levels in the body. Histamine is what causes many of the symptoms of an allergic reaction.
- **Bronchodilators** (e.g., Ventolin, Atrovent, Bricanyl) are inhaled medications used to stop an asthma-like response and to open airways to improve breathing.
- **Corticosteroids** (e.g., prednisone, Solu-Medrol, Pediapred) are strong anti-inflammatory medications used to help settle and prevent relapse in severe allergic reactions.
- **Decongestants** (e.g., Triaminic, Dimetapp) are used to reduce swelling of the mucous membranes (such as nasal and sinus swelling) in allergic reactions.

ALLERGIC REACTIONS

BABY IS CRYING

Elizabeth was seven months old when her mother brought her to the emergency department.

"She has been crying for two hours!" her exasperated mother proclaimed. "No matter what I do she won't stop crying. I have fed her, burped her and changed her, but she just keeps crying! She is usually such a good baby but tonight she is just uncontrollable. She has been completely healthy up until now without even a cold."

I reviewed with mom a top-down approach in examining every part of the baby's body. Indeed, Elizabeth was a healthy but not a happy baby. The examination was completely normal except for a small piece of thread from her baby blanket that had somehow wound itself around her finger. This small piece of thread was cutting off the circulation to Elizabeth's finger and making it swell and turn blue at the tip.

Removal of this thread caused Elizabeth to immediately stop crying and, shortly thereafter, fall asleep.

The crying of a baby is like the screech of car tires:
it makes you stop, look and listen.

The knack of parenthood includes learning to interpret your
baby's different cries.

BABY IS CRYING

BABY IS CRYING

SYMPTOMS

- Uncontrolled or prolonged crying (more than two hours)
- Baby will not settle and cannot be comforted

GOALS

To determine and treat the cause of discomfort.

TIPS

- When your baby shows one or more of the following symptoms,
  chances are he or she has become sick and needs treatment:
  listless or unresponsive (not smiling); crying excessively; not eating;
  cries despite comforting; breathing rapidly; fever; cannot sit or stand
  (except infants); whimpering; will not play or sleep; rubs ears constantly;
  looks pale or sweaty; cannot be awakened.
- Take off all clothes and check each body part. Check for tight clothes
  or an open diaper pin. Is baby too hot or too cold?
- Look for signs of illness – cold, cough, rash, vomiting, diarrhea,
  constipation, thrush, stuffy or runny nose, stomach ache, fever.
- Teething (see page 105) is a common problem that is hard to identify.
- Babies need love, attention and comforting, especially when ill.
  It is not possible to spoil your child in the first six months of life.
  Comforting tips include: reducing stimuli, such as sound and light;
  playing quiet music, singing, talking softly, rocking, rubbing stomach,
  warm bath, holding your baby.
- Crying is your baby's way of trying to tell you something.
  Listen to the cry. Is baby angry? Scared? Hungry? In pain? Frustrated?
  Try to learn the subtle differences in your baby's cries.
- A sick baby often shows a change in appetite, activity and/or attitude.
  Watch for these changes.

BABY IS CRYING

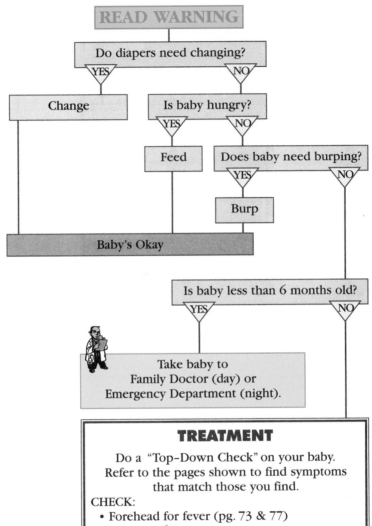

READ WARNING

Do diapers need changing?
- YES → Change
- NO → Is baby hungry?
  - YES → Feed
  - NO → Does baby need burping?
    - YES → Burp
    - NO →

Change, Feed, Burp → **Baby's Okay**

Is baby less than 6 months old?
- YES → Take baby to Family Doctor (day) or Emergency Department (night).
- NO → TREATMENT

TREATMENT

Do a "Top-Down Check" on your baby.
Refer to the pages shown to find symptoms
that match those you find.

CHECK:
- Forehead for fever (pg. 73 & 77)
- Eyes (pg. 69)
- Ears (pg. 65)
- Nose (pg. 29 & 93)
- Mouth (pg. 41, 105 & 109)
- Chest (pg. 25, 41 & 49)
- Stomach (pg. 33, 37, 61, 97 & 113)
- Diaper area (pg. 57)
- Skin (pg. 17, 45 & 85)
- Arms and legs (p. 53)

WARNING: Infants under 6 months of age are at a higher risk,
even with minor ailments. Follow Treatment cautiously and
seek medical attention if your child's symptoms do not improve.

BABY IS CRYING

Trade Secrets

- A crying child can instill chaos even in the most organized homes. For this reason, you must have an organized, systematic approach when dealing with this parental dilemma.
- New babies are often unsettled for 2 – 4 hours per day and approximately one day per week. This is considered normal.
- Babies are often unsettled in the evenings. Often 5 pm to 9 pm. This is considered the 'witching hours' for babies

Definitions

- Listless means lacking in energy or spirit.
- Parents' Intuition refers to the innate ability or sixth sense of all parents to know when something is wrong with their child.
- Prolonged Crying refers to crying that lasts longer than two hours without resolution and especially if such crying is out of character for the baby.
- Top-Down Check refers to the systematic approach of reviewing each body part and system in a child to determine a cause of crying, starting from the top of the head and proceeding to the tips of the toes.

Synonyms

- Bawling
- Sobbing
- Weeping

Medications/Treatments

- Medications depend upon the cause of the crying.
- **Acetaminophen Infant Drops** (e.g., Tempra, Tylenol) are used to both control pain and lower fever. *Do not use ASA or aspirin.*
- **Anti-inflammatories** (Childrens Motrin, Childrens Advil) are used to treat pain, fever and inflammation

BABY IS CRYING

BRONCHIOLITIS

CASE STUDY

Matthew was only six months old when he was brought in to the emergency department at 3 am one February night.

"He hasn't been sleeping well for the past two nights," his father reported. "What started out like a regular cold now seems to be causing some breathing trouble. I spent the last 20 minutes walking up and down the driveway with him. That and the trip here seem to have improved things somewhat. He is normally a very happy baby but the last two days he has been miserable and wants to be held all the time. What really brought us in tonight is his noisy breathing, and he has been coughing to the point of vomiting. He has started grunting and wheezing, and his lips turned a little blue tonight after one of his coughing attacks."

On examination Matthew had a clear runny nose, a steady, recurrent cough and was breathing at 48 breaths a minute. He also had some chest retractions (sucking in of chest and stomach) when breathing in.

"Oh, by the way, his two-year-old brother was just in hospital with Respiratory Syncytial Virus (RSV) bronchiolitis two weeks ago," Matthew's father added.

Matthew was admitted to hospital that night and was subsequently found to have, and was treated for RSV bronchiolitis like his brother.

Bronchiolitis is like asthma for the pediatric crowd.

Being a parent can be a lot like watching a horror movie.
Although you can usually anticipate the scary parts,
they can still scare the hell out of you.
Bronchiolitis can be one of the "parental scary parts."

BRONCHIOLITIS

SYMPTOMS

- Cold and cough symptoms that after two to three days suddenly get worse
- Breathing fast and with difficulty
(asthma-like symptoms, coughing and wheezing)

GOALS

Treat symptoms until bronchial infection clears and breathing improves.

TIPS

- Usually occurs in winter and lasts seven to 10 days, like a cold. Treatment is for fever and cold symptoms (see Fever and Colds sections).
- Children with bronchiolitis are treated like asthmatics and are more likely to develop asthma later in life.(About half develop asthma).
- Try warm, clear fluids to reduce coughing spasms.
- DO NOT allow smoking around your child.
- A cold air vaporizer helps some children. Discontinue use if it seems to make coughing or wheezing worse.
- Symptoms of wheezing and difficulty breathing usually worsen for the first two to five days, then improve.
- A blocked nose in infants under nine months can cause feeding problems. Use saline nose drops and a nasal suction bulb to clear. Do one nostril at a time. See doctor if feeding is still poor after cleaning the nasal passages.
- Respiratory Syncytial Virus is spread through infected secretions from an infected person. Wash your hands well whenever treating a child with an infection.
- Children with underlying medical conditions may develop a more severe disease and must be watched closely.

BRONCHIOLITIS

BRONCHIOLITIS

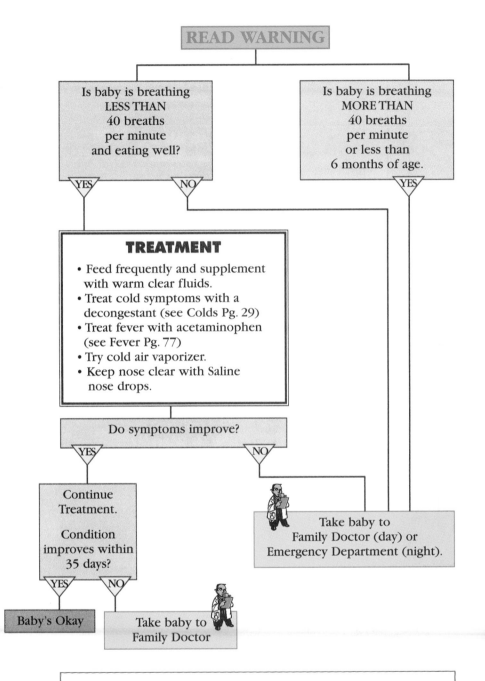

READ WARNING

Is baby is breathing
LESS THAN
40 breaths
per minute
and eating well?

Is baby is breathing
MORE THAN
40 breaths
per minute
or less than
6 months of age.

YES

NO

YES

TREATMENT

• Feed frequently and supplement
  with warm clear fluids.
• Treat cold symptoms with a
  decongestant (see Colds Pg. 29)
• Treat fever with acetaminophen
  (see Fever Pg. 77)
• Try cold air vaporizer.
• Keep nose clear with Saline
  nose drops.

Do symptoms improve?

YES

NO

Continue
Treatment.

Condition
improves within
35 days?

Take baby to
Family Doctor (day) or
Emergency Department (night).

YES

NO

Baby's Okay

Take baby to
Family Doctor

SIGNS OF DEHYDRATION:
• Dry mouth and tongue • Cracked lips • No tears • Sunken eyes
• No urine in six hours (or fewer than six diapers per day)
• Depressed soft spot on scalp • Lethargic
(See pg. 63 for more on dehydration)

BRONCHIOLITIS

BRONCHIOLITIS

Trade Secrets

- Bronchiolitis often occurs in winter and spring epidemics.
- Bronchiolitis has the same symptoms as a regular cold in an older child or adult. Symptoms will usually be more severe the younger the child.
- Bronchiolitis is usually worst in the first two to three days.
- Bronchiolitis is most common in babies 6 to 9 months old.

Definitions

- **Bronchiolitis** is the inflammation of the bronchioles (small breathing tubes) in the lungs. It is caused by a virus. Antibiotics are of no use in treatment.
- **Retraction** refers to the sucking in of the chest or stomach when breathing in.
- **Wheezing** is a musical, whistling sound usually made while breathing out and caused when the airways are restricted.
- **RSV** (Respiratory Syncytial Virus) is one of the commonest causes of bronchiolitis. It usually causes bronchiolitis from October to March.
- **Inhaled** means to breathe in.
- **Injected** means to have a needle.
- **Oral** means taken by mouth.
- **Vaporizers** are also called steamers or humidifiers, and are used to increase the humidity in the air.

Synonyms

- Infectious asthma

Medications/Treatments

- **Acetaminophen Infant Drops** (e.g., Tempra, Tylenol) are used to both control pain and lower a fever. Do not use ASA or aspirin.
- **Antiviral Medications** (e.g., Ribavirin) are an inhaled antiviral agent for the treatment of severe cases of bronchiolitis. Pregnant women should avoid exposure.
- **Bronchodilators** (e.g., albuterol, salbutamol, ipratropium) are inhaled medications used to stop asthma-like attacks and open airways to improve breathing.
- **Corticosteroids** (e.g., Solu-Medrol, prednisone, Pulmicort) are anti-inflammatory medications sometimes used to heal inflamed airways.
- **Decongestants or Antihistamine-Decongestants** (e.g., Dimetapp oral infant drops, Triaminic oral infant drops) are used to relieve nasal and sinus congestion and postnasal drip. Do not administer decongestants or antihistamines in children less than 6 months old without first consulting your family doctor.
- **Oxygen** is used to assist in breathing.
- **Cold air vaporizers** are used to add humidity to the air.
- **Saline nose drops** are used to clear and moisturize nasal passages.

BRONCHIOLITIS

COLDS

Justin was seven months old when he was brought to the office.

"He just hasn't been himself for the past few days," said his mother. "Usually he is such a good eater, but now he isn't eating well and he doesn't even want his apple juice. Last night was the last straw. He didn't sleep well and he seems to be having trouble breathing through his nose."

On examination, this usually bright and curious boy looked miserable. He was clinging to his mother and had watery eyes and a red, runny nose. He was sneezing and had an occasional wet cough. He was also running a fever of 38°C (100°F) that his mother told me had come and gone during the past two days. He was having no difficulty breathing and had no skin rashes.

"His six-year-old brother brought the same thing home from school last week," his mother explained.

Justin was experiencing his first cold.

A child's frequency of colds should improve like a golf score. As a beginner it's quite high, but in time, the score should drop.

COLDS

COLDS

SYMPTOMS

- Runny or stuffy nose • Sneezing and coughing
- Low-grade fever (less than 38.5°C or 101.3°F) • Watery eyes
- Tiredness and loss of appetite

GOALS

Make baby comfortable while the body fights the virus.

TIPS

- Comforting ideas: dress baby comfortably, wipe eyes, feed frequent small meals, use cool air vaporizer. Clean the vaporizer daily.
- Continue regular feeding and encourage baby to drink plenty of extra clear liquids. Warm fluids are less likely to cause coughing, but use whatever the child will take.
- Coughing is the way babies clear their throats.
Do not suppress a cough unless directed to by your family doctor.
- If coughing is the main symptom, see Coughs, page 41.
- Try to keep the nose clear. Try administering saline nose drops while baby is feeding and / or use a nasal suction bulb.
- Decongestant nose drops may be of value in keeping the nose open. Check with your doctor for his / her suggestions.
- Wash your hands well and avoid touching your nose, mouth or eyes when exposed to someone with a cold.
This will help prevent transmission to someone else.
- Treat fever and discomfort with acetaminophen.

COLDS

COLDS

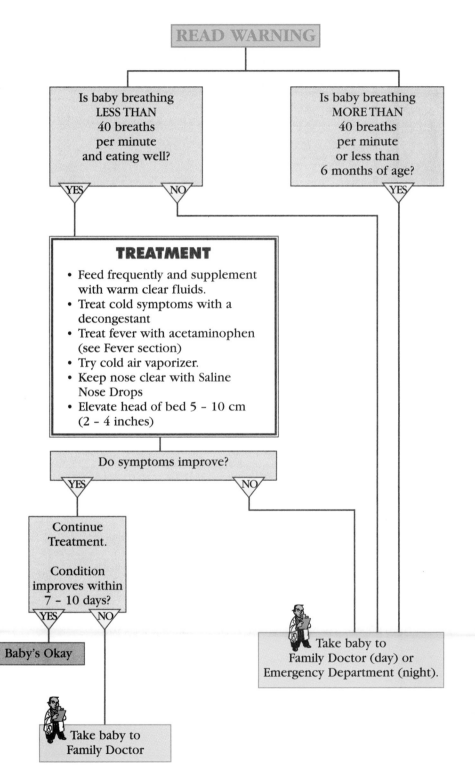

Is baby breathing
LESS THAN
40 breaths
per minute
and eating well?

YES   NO

Is baby breathing
MORE THAN
40 breaths
per minute
or less than
6 months of age?

YES

TREATMENT

- Feed frequently and supplement with warm clear fluids.
- Treat cold symptoms with a decongestant
- Treat fever with acetaminophen (see Fever section)
- Try cold air vaporizer.
- Keep nose clear with Saline Nose Drops
- Elevate head of bed 5 - 10 cm (2 - 4 inches)

Do symptoms improve?

YES   NO

Continue Treatment.

Condition improves within 7 - 10 days?

YES   NO

Baby's Okay

Take baby to
Family Doctor (day) or
Emergency Department (night).

Take baby to
Family Doctor

COLDS

Trade Secrets

- It is normal for otherwise healthy preschool children to acquire anywhere from six to 12 colds per year.
  Children with older, school age siblings or children who are attending daycare may have even more colds than this!
- Do not use antibiotics for colds. Colds are viral infections against which antibiotics are useless. Unnecessary use of antibiotics exposes your baby to potential adverse effects and leads to resistant diseases.

Definitions

- **Colds** are viral infections of the nasal and upper airway passages.
- **Listless** means lacking interest in doing regular activities.
- **Low-grade Fever** is a thermometer reading of less than 38.5°C or 101.3°F.
- **Mucus** is a clear to white nasal discharge.
- **Nasal Discharge** is the substance secreted from the nose.
- **Vaporizers** are also called steamers or humidifiers, and are used to increase the humidity in the air.

Synonyms

- Common cold
- Upper respiratory infection
- Upper respiratory tract infection
- Often wrongly called the flu

Medications/Treatments

- **Acetaminophen Infant Drops** (e.g., Tempra, Tylenol) are used to both control pain and lower a fever. Do not use ASA or aspirin.
- **Cold air vaporizers** are used to add humidity to the air.
- **Decongestants or Antihistamine-Decongestants**
  (e.g., Dimetapp oral infant drops, Triaminic oral infant drops) are used to relieve nasal and sinus congestion and postnasal drip. Do not administer decongestants or antihistamines in children less than 6 months old without first consulting your family doctor.
- **Decongestant nose drops** are used to open blocked nasal passages but, check with your family doctor prior to using them.
- **Saline Nose Drops** (e.g., Otrivin saline drops, Salinex) provide relief from dry and irritated nasal passages by moisturizing as well as thinning out thick nasal mucus.

COLDS

COLIC

Jeremy was two months old when he was brought in to the office.

His parents looked exhausted. They hadn't slept for two nights. "We just don't know what else to do," his parents said. "There must be something wrong, he's crying all the time. The only way we can get him to settle is to take him for a ride in the van."

The parents went on to explain that their child had them at their wits' end. He was eating well but seemed irritable and fussy most of the time, especially from 6 to 9 pm. At this time of night, every night, he became an inconsolable, fist-clenching, back-arching demon. Nothing they tried would settle him. He would often draw up his legs and have what they felt may be increased gas and stomach cramps during these periods of inconsolability.

They were feeding and changing him correctly, and developmentally he was doing well. My examination revealed a perfectly healthy infant.

Jeremy had colic.

Getting through the challenge of a child with colic
is much like quitting smoking.
Often the psychological trauma is worse
than the physical demands.

COLIC

COLIC

SYMPTOMS

- Unexplained crying in a healthy baby less than three months old
- Fussiness or irritability, lasting two to three hours, usually in the evening

GOALS

Rule out the possibility of more serious illness and maintain a loving, patient attitude. Remember: Babies at this age cannot be "spoiled."

TIPS

- If breast feeding, do not stop. Get help from your doctor, breast feeding support group or a lactation consultant.
- If breast feeding, monitor how your diet affects your baby (especially watch milk, chocolate, caffeine, spices, alcohol, vegetables).
- If formula feeding, talk with your doctor about changing your formula.
- Visit your family doctor regularly during this time. Make sure that your baby is gaining weight and developing normally.
- Use the Top-Down approach flow chart on page 23 to eliminate other illnesses or causes of pain.
- Baby will usually settle when held or comforted. Try car rides or rocking in a chair, cradle or swing. Soothing music will often help.
- Colic can drive even the most patient parent crazy, because nothing seems to work. Joined with the newness of the child and the associated sleep deprivation, an inconsolable infant is a daunting task. The secret is to *Get Help, Get Out, Get Focused*.
  Get Help: Use your friends and family liberally during these times.
  Get Out: You must have a chance to get out without the baby, regroup and get your perspective back again.
  Get Focused: The most important things during this turbulent time are your health and that of your infant, not the housework.

COLIC

COLIC

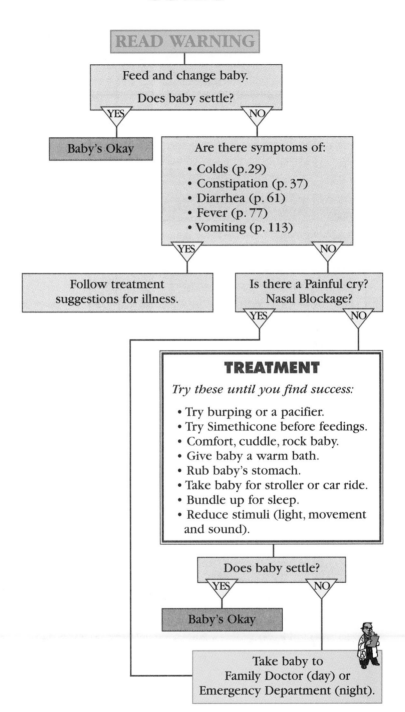

READ WARNING

Feed and change baby.

Does baby settle?

YES — Baby's Okay

NO — Are there symptoms of:
- Colds (p.29)
- Constipation (p. 37)
- Diarrhea (p. 61)
- Fever (p. 77)
- Vomiting (p. 113)

YES — Follow treatment suggestions for illness.

NO — Is there a Painful cry? Nasal Blockage?

YES →

NO →

TREATMENT

Try these until you find success:

- Try burping or a pacifier.
- Try Simethicone before feedings.
- Comfort, cuddle, rock baby.
- Give baby a warm bath.
- Rub baby's stomach.
- Take baby for stroller or car ride.
- Bundle up for sleep.
- Reduce stimuli (light, movement and sound).

Does baby settle?

YES — Baby's Okay

NO — Take baby to Family Doctor (day) or Emergency Department (night).

IMPORTANT
If baby is no better after 3 hours, or if you are afraid of losing control, GET HELP

COLIC

COLIC

Trade Secrets

- About 10 percent of babies have colic. It is not a sign of bad parenting.
- True colic starts in the first month and is gone by the fourth month.
- Some colicky babies respond to sound and some only to silence.
- Babies normally cry about two hours a day at two weeks;
  3 hours a day at six weeks; and roughly 1 hour per day by 12 weeks.
- Colicky children are usually extremely sensitive to stimulation.
- Have your family doctor rule out more serious conditions before deciding that your baby has colic.

Definitions

- **Colic** is a poorly understood condition of excessive crying in the first three months of life in otherwise healthy children.
- **Top-Down Check** refers to the systematic approach of reviewing each body part and system in a child to determine a cause of crying.

Synonyms

- None

Medications/Treatments

- **Acetaminophen Infant Drops** (e.g., Tempra, Tylenol) are used to both control pain and lower a fever. Do not use ASA or aspirin.
- **Simethicone** (e.g., Ovol, Phazyme) is a medication used to reduce gas and abdominal cramps.
- **Colick-No-More** is a new appliance that attaches to the crib and stimulates the movement of a car ride. This appliance may be invaluable to parents with colicky babies.

COLIC

CONSTIPATION

Hyung was 18 months old when his mom brought him in to the office.

"He now cries every time he tries to have a bowel movement," his worried mother began. "His habits used to be quite normal but now he only has a bowel movement every four or five days. Yesterday I noticed a little streak of blood in his diaper after he passed a particularly hard stool. He's just not himself the last little while. His appetite has never been great but now all he will drink is milk, and he will only eat cheese and bananas."

Examination showed a healthy boy with the start of an anal fissure (a small cut in the rectum). I also discovered that Hyung's new baby sister had recently been brought home from the hospital.

Hyung had developed constipation, likely caused in part by his diet, as well as by the stress of sharing his parents with his new sister.

Your digestive system is like the septic system at the cottage: if you feed it the wrong things it doesn't take long to plug up.

Constipation is our bowels way of telling us to get back to the basics. More fruits and fruit juices, vegetables, fibre-rich foods, bran, water and exercise.

CONSTIPATION

CONSTIPATION

SYMPTOMS

• Hard, dry stool • Bowel movements are painful or difficult to pass
• They may be infrequent as a result

GOALS

Define and recognize true constipation, and take steps to correct safely.

TIPS

• Causes can include: not enough fluid or fibre in diet (including too strong a formula mix), illness, inadequate activity. Use the dietary suggestions below only when the child is of appropriate age.
• Increase fluids by giving prune, pear, grape or apple juice mixed with an equal amount of water. Milk is not considered a fluid.
• Fibre or "roughage" is found in certain fruits (prunes, pears, apricots, plums, peaches, dates, raisins); certain vegetables (peas, beans, broccoli, lettuce, cabbage); whole grain breads, cereals and pastas.
• Reduce bananas, apples, squash, carrots, white rice, cereal, cheese, dairy products and foods high in sugar content.
• For a child who is neither breastfed nor bottlefed (likely over one year of age) you must:
  • Increase fruit, fruit juices and vegetables. Often raw fruit and vegetables are best. Avoid foods your child has difficulty chewing or swallowing.
  • Increase fibre or bran in the diet. This includes fibre-rich cereals, cookies, muffins and biscuits. Add bran to foods.
  • Have your child drink more water or very diluted juices.
  • Encourage physical activity and play (especially if your child tends to be less active).
  • Reduce cow's milk and other dairy products. You may wish to return to formula if you recently switched to cow's milk.

CONSTIPATION

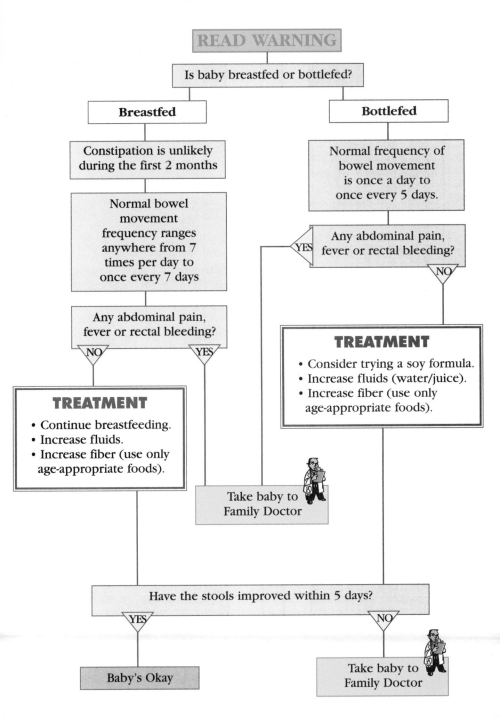

READ WARNING

Is baby breastfed or bottlefed?

Breastfed

Constipation is unlikely during the first 2 months

Normal bowel movement frequency ranges anywhere from 7 times per day to once every 7 days

Any abdominal pain, fever or rectal bleeding?

NO   YES

TREATMENT
• Continue breastfeeding.
• Increase fluids.
• Increase fiber (use only age-appropriate foods).

Bottlefed

Normal frequency of bowel movement is once a day to once every 5 days.

YES   Any abdominal pain, fever or rectal bleeding?

NO

TREATMENT
• Consider trying a soy formula.
• Increase fluids (water/juice).
• Increase fiber (use only age-appropriate foods).

Take baby to Family Doctor

Have the stools improved within 5 days?

YES   NO

Baby's Okay

Take baby to Family Doctor

CONSTIPATION

CONSTIPATION

Trade Secrets

- Infants straining to pass a constipated stool can sometimes be helped by:
  - Helping them draw up their legs or squat.
  - Put them in a warm bath to help the passage of the stool.
- Constipation is passing hard, dry stool. It refers to the consistency, discomfort and difficulty of bowel movements, not the frequency.
- Babies often grunt, pull up their legs and become flushed when passing a stool. This may be normal. Crying during the passing of a bowel movement is not normal.
- Constipation is very rare in breast-fed babies.
- Constipation usually occurs around times of diet changes (i.e., adding solid foods or switching to cow's milk) or during times of change or stress at home.

Definitions

- **Anal Fissure** is a small crack or tear in the rectum as a result of the passage of a large or hard stool.
- **Constipation** is the infrequent passage of hard, dry stool.
- **Enema** is an introduction of a solution into the rectum to promote clearing of the bowel. This works best to clear the lower bowel.
- **Fiber Foods** are those high in roughage (e.g., unmilled bran).
- **Laxatives** are medications used to stimulate the bowel to move and pass stool.
- **Stools/Bowel movement** (e.g., poo, feces)

Synonyms

- Plugged up
- Bunged up

Medications/Treatments

- The use of all medications, softeners, laxatives and enemas should be avoided unless directed by your doctor. This includes herbal and naturopathic products.

CONSTIPATION

COUGHS

CASE STUDY

Julie was 18 months old when she was brought in to the emergency department on a December evening.

"She has been coughing off and on for the past week," her father said. "It seems to be especially bad when she's in the house. Other than the cough, she has been eating well and seems healthy enough except for a slight runny nose and itchy eyes, again only when she is inside. When we take her out of the house, she is fine."

Examination revealed a healthy and happy girl with minor redness of her mucous membranes. There was no fever or difficulty breathing. There was no coughing during the examination. Further questions to Julie's father uncovered that there were no new pets, construction on or other changes to the house. However, we did discover that both mom and dad each smoked approximately a pack of cigarettes a day.

When her mom and dad agreed to refrain from smoking inside the house, Julie's cough disappeared.

"Quote"

Coughing is the lungs' way of taking out the trash.

Smoking is one of the most common irritants to children, seconded only by parents.

Smoking and coughing go together like coffee and doughnuts.

COUGHS

COUGHS

SYMPTOMS
- An attempt by the body to expel something from the respiratory tract

GOALS
Determine the type and severity of cough and treat accordingly.

TIPS

- Coughing is a natural process for clearing the throat or lungs of infection, mucus, etc. It is the way a baby clears its throat.
- Avoid cough suppressants unless directed by a doctor, or baby is unable to sleep because of coughing, or is coughing to the point of vomiting.
- A warm room, cold air vaporizer and increasing fluid intake can help.
- To reduce nighttime coughing, raise the head of the bed 5–10 centimeters (2–4 inches).
- Coughing may be a sign of allergies or asthma.
- Croupy coughs (hoarse, barky, seal-sounding coughs) may be improved by taking a warmly dressed child into the cooler outside air.
- Cigarette smoke is a very common cause of infant coughing. DO NOT SMOKE anywhere near a baby.
- Warm (not hot) fluids are less likely to stimulate cough. Try warm, diluted tea mixed with a 1/2 teaspoon of honey or corn syrup. Do not use honey in babies under one year of age. Corn syrup may be substituted in this age group.
- Use acetaminophen for pain and fever.
- Do not give babies cough lozenges (candies).
- Lifting baby from a lying position to rest on your shoulder may reduce coughing.

COUGHS

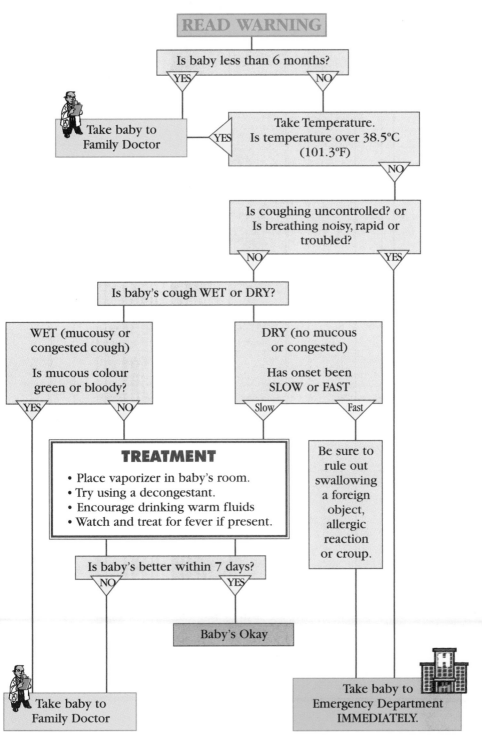

Is baby less than 6 months?

YES — NO

Take baby to Family Doctor

YES

Take Temperature. Is temperature over 38.5°C (101.3°F)

NO

Is coughing uncontrolled? or Is breathing noisy, rapid or troubled?

NO — YES

Is baby's cough WET or DRY?

WET (mucousy or congested cough)

Is mucous colour green or bloody?

YES — NO

DRY (no mucous or congested)

Has onset been SLOW or FAST

Slow — Fast

TREATMENT

- Place vaporizer in baby's room.
- Try using a decongestant.
- Encourage drinking warm fluids
- Watch and treat for fever if present.

Be sure to rule out swallowing a foreign object, allergic reaction or croup.

Is baby's better within 7 days?

NO — YES

Baby's Okay

Take baby to Family Doctor

Take baby to Emergency Department IMMEDIATELY.

COUGHS

COUGHS

Trade Secrets

- By far the most common causes of coughing in the under-two age group are infections, irritants (e.g., passive smoke) and reactive airway disease (asthma). It is for this reason that many will end up at the family doctor for treatment.
- Cough suppressants should be discouraged unless directed by your family doctor.
- In order to stop the cough you need to first determine then treat the cause.

Definitions

- **Dry Cough** is a cough that does not produce sputum (spit).
- **Labored Breathing** means difficulty or hard work when breathing.
- **Onset of Cough** refers to how fast it has developed – fast is within minutes, slow is within hours to days.
- **Reactive Airway Disease** (RAD) is a condition characterized by increased mucus production, inflamed and narrowed airways and wheezing and /or coughing.
- **Mucus** is spit or sputum from the throat and lungs.
  Green, brown or bloody sputum is usually caused by infection.
- **Uncontrolled Coughing** is persistent or continuous coughing. Coughing of this type often leads to the point of vomiting.
- **Wet Cough** is a cough that produces sputum (spit).

Synonyms

- Hacking
- Barking

Medications/Treatments

- **Decongestants or Antihistamine-Decongestants** (e.g., Dimetapp oral infant drops, Triaminic oral infant drops) are used to relieve nasal and sinus congestion and postnasal drip. Do not administer decongestants or antihistamines in children less than 6 months old without first consulting your family doctor.
- **Cough Suppressants** (e.g., Benylin, Koffex, Delsym) are used to stop cough. Many have a combination of medicines – read the label.
- **Vaporizers**, also called steamers or humidifiers, are used to increase the humidity in the air.

COUGHS

CRADLE CAP

Jonathan was one month old when he was brought in to the office.

"He seems to have cradle cap," his mother told me. "It was kind of dry and flaky so my neighbor told me to stop shampooing and to rub it with baby oil, but it just seems to be getting worse. Now he is starting to get these thick yellow patches on his scalp."

On examination Jonathan had some mild redness of the scalp with some flaking of the skin. The skin was shiny from the oiliness. Some thick, yellow, greasy plaques had started to form on the top of the scalp. There was also some redness and flaking of the skin on the forehead and around the eyebrows.

Jonathan had a case of cradle cap.

Cradle cap is an oil problem and therefore doesn't need an oil solution.

Putting oil on cradle cap is like putting gasoline on a fire. It usually makes the matter worse.

CRADLE CAP

SYMPTOMS

- Mild symptoms include dry, flaky skin on baby's scalp
- Severe symptoms include thick, greasy and scaly plaques

GOALS

Determine whether symptoms are mild or severe and treat accordingly.

TIPS

- Cradle cap is a type of seborrheic dermatitis very common in children under 18 months of age.
- Baby may have associated rashes in the eyebrows, behind the ears and in skin folds.
- This is a type of oil problem. Therefore, oil is not used except to loosen thickened plaques as directed in the flow chart.
- Shampoo daily with a mild baby shampoo.
- Gently brush the scalp daily with a baby brush to loosen scales / plaques and stimulate skin growth.
- For severe cases of cradle cap, with thick dry skin plaques, apply mineral oil to the plaques overnight and shampoo off in the morning.
- There are special shampoos, lotions and creams available for difficult cases. See your family doctor for a prescription.
- Do not use anti-dandruff shampoos without the advice of your family doctor.
- Some yeast likes to live in oil, so treatment often includes both oil removal and treatment for a yeast infection.

CRADLE CAP

CRADLE CAP

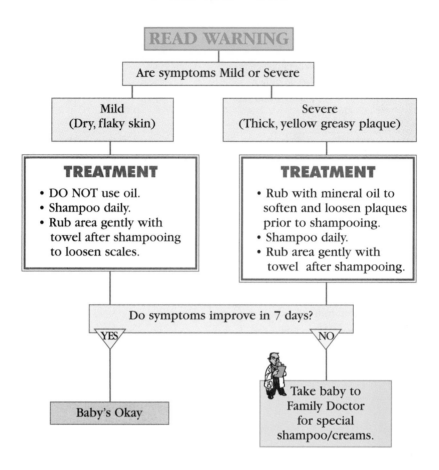

READ WARNING

Are symptoms Mild or Severe

Mild
(Dry, flaky skin)

Severe
(Thick, yellow greasy plaque)

TREATMENT

• DO NOT use oil.
• Shampoo daily.
• Rub area gently with towel after shampooing to loosen scales.

TREATMENT

• Rub with mineral oil to soften and loosen plaques prior to shampooing.
• Shampoo daily.
• Rub area gently with towel after shampooing.

Do symptoms improve in 7 days?

YES

NO

Baby's Okay

Take baby to Family Doctor for special shampoo/creams.

Infant skin conditions are difficult to diagnose
without seeing them.
If in doubt about a skin condition,
see your Family Doctor.

CRADLE CAP

Trade Secrets

- Persistence in treatment is the name of the game with cradle cap. Shampoo and brush hair / scalp daily.
- Keep in mind that this is a self-limiting condition. It usually resolves itself within the first year of a child's life.

Definitions

- **Cradle Cap** is really seborrheic dermatitis, a pediatric skin condition caused by excessive skin oiliness. It usually involves the scalp but may also involve the face, eyebrows, behind the ears and skin creases.
- **Plaques** are flat patches from the buildup of skin flakes.

Synonyms

- Seborrhea
- Seborrheic dermatitis
- Baby dandruff

Medications/Treatments

- **Baby Shampoo** (e.g., Johnson's Baby Shampoo, Baby Magic, Baby's Own) removes the oil from the scalp.
- **Mineral Oil** (e.g., baby oil, mineral oil) is used only in severe cases with thick plaques on the scalp.
- **Topical Steroid** (e.g., hydrocortisone) lotions, creams or ointments are often used for more resistant areas.
- **Specialized Shampoos** (e.g., sulfur, salicyclic acid and ketoconazole [Nizoral]) may be prescribed by your family doctor for more resistant cases.

CRADLE CAP

CROUP

Brent was 17 months old when he was brought in to the emergency department at 4 am on a January morning.

"He has had a cold for three days," his weary father reported. "Now we can't get him to stop this terrible-sounding cough. The more upset he gets, the worse the cough. I bundled him up and walked with him up and down our driveway for the past 30 minutes. That and the trip here seem to have helped the most. He also seems to have developed a mild fever and a hoarse voice."

Brent's distinctive seal-like cough could be heard throughout the department. He was also having some difficulty breathing in. He had some retraction of his chest wall when he inhaled and had a breathing rate of 56 breaths per minute. He did not have any drooling, fever or stridor during the exam.

Brent had croup. He was admitted to the hospital for treatment.

Any time that your child starts making sounds that can be described as any animal, other than human, it is time to see the doctor.

CROUP

CROUP

SYMPTOMS

- Distinctive harsh, barking cough (sounds like a seal) and hoarse voice
- May also have cold symptoms (sneezing, runny nose, fever, watery eyes, etc.)
or difficulty breathing

GOALS

Treat symptoms and watch carefully for any breathing problems
until the infection is gone.

TIPS

- Croup usually occurs in spring or fall and lasts three to five days.
- Croup can be dangerous. It is usually worse at night. Consider sleeping
next to the child to monitor the severity of the croup.
- Encourage child to take clear fluids if possible.
- Give warm (not hot) fluids to help the cough. Antibiotics are of
no use for viral croup and should be avoided.
- Use a cold air vaporizer (add ice to the water, if possible).
Bundle baby and make room steamy and cool for all bed times.
If no vaporizer is available, take baby with you into a steamy bathroom
or shower. Do this at least four times a day for 15 minutes each time.
- Watch for fever and treat with acetaminophen infant drops as directed.
- Treat cold symptoms (see Colds, page 29).
- Crying will make it worse. Try to settle your baby.
- Try bundling baby and take outside if weather is cool. In cool weather,
children often improve on the way to the emergency department because
cold air shrinks inflamed passages and relieves breathing difficulty.
- DO NOT SMOKE around a baby with croup.

CROUP

CROUP

READ WARNING

CHECK FOR STRIDOR

1. Stridor is a harsh sound heard when a baby is breathing in.
2. Especially prominent when coughing, crying or upset.
3. Often associated with rapid breathing (more than 40 breaths per minute).
4. Often associated with indrawing (sucking in) of the chest when breathing in.

IS STRIDOR PRESENT?

YES / NO

Take baby to Emergency Department IMMEDIATELY.

TREATMENT

- Take outside into cooler air.
- Place vaporizer in room.
- Treat fever with Acetaminophen Infant Drops.
- Treat cold symptoms with Decongestant.

Symptoms worsen or stridor develops.

Symptoms improve.

Take baby to Emergency Department IMMEDIATELY.

Continue treatment for maximum of 5 days.

Are symptoms gone?

YES / NO

Baby's Okay

Take baby to Family Doctor.

CROUP

CROUP

Trade Secrets

- Croup generally affects children between three months and three years.
- Any condition that affects the breathing of a child should be watched very closely.
- A doctor should see any condition that produces an unusual cough or breathing characteristics.
- The secret in treating croup is to treat early and treat aggressively.
- Cool, humidified air is the first step in the croup treatment plan.

Definitions

- **Croup** is a viral illness causing a narrowing of the subglottic region (under the vocal cords). This is the narrowest part of a child's airway and may, therefore, cause breathing difficulties.
- **Croup Tents** are used in some hospitals to increase the humidity and oxygen in the air the child is breathing. Mask / hose treatment is used in many hospitals as an alternative to croup tents because they allow more movement by the child.
- **Stridor** is a harsh vibrating sound made when breathing in.
- **Vaporizer** is another name for a steamer, cold air vaporizer or humidifier. It is used to increase the humidity in a room.

Synonyms

- Acute viral croup
- Episodic croup
- Laryngotracheobronchitis (LTB)
- Viral croup

Medications/Treatments

- **Acetaminophen Infant Drops** (e.g., Tempra, Tylenol) are used to both control pain and lower a fever. Do not use ASA or aspirin.
- **Decongestants or Antihistamine-Decongestants** (e.g., Dimetapp Oral Infant Drops, Triaminic Oral Infant Drops) are used to relieve nasal and sinus congestion and postnasal drip. Do not administer decongestants or antihistamines in children less than 6 months old without first consulting your family doctor.
- **Corticosteroids** (e.g., Decadron, Pulmicort, Pediapred) are anti-inflammatory medications used in more severe cases.
- **Racemic Epinephrine** (e.g., Vaponefrin) is a hospital treatment to relieve the airway obstruction by shrinking the swelling in the airways.

CROUP

CUTS & ABRASIONS

Tyler was 24 months when he was brought in to the emergency department.

"He was running outside when he slipped and fell in the gravel," his mother said. "He has cuts and scrapes to his hands and knees."

On further questioning, I determined that Tyler had not knocked himself out as a result of the fall, nor had he vomited following the fall. His immunizations were also up-to-date.

On examination, Tyler had large scrapes on both knees that needed cleaning to remove the gravel, as well as a small but deep cut on his hand. Because the cut continued to bleed despite the application of pressure on the wound, it required cleaning and stitches (sutures).

Cuts and abrasions in children are like kids and dogs: inseparable.

As a parent, you will definitely need a good grounding in basic first aid.

CUTS & ABRASIONS

SYMPTOMS

A break or tear in the surface of the skin.

GOALS

Keep the wound clean so that it will heal naturally.

TIPS

- Cuts and abrasions are very common in the first two years of life, especially when babies are learning to walk.
- Washing at least twice a day with a mild soap and water is the cheapest and safest way to keep a wound clean. Wash wound for five minutes.
- Trim off any small pieces of loose skin.
- During the day, apply an antibiotic ointment and cover the wound to protect from contamination.
- Use non-stick dressings if available in your drug store (e.g., Telfa).
- DO NOT use alcohol, iodine, mercurochrome or hydrogen peroxide on a baby's wound.
- At night, leave the wound uncovered to air dry, unless bleeding or drainage is occurring.
- Check to ensure tetanus shots are up-to-date.
- If stitches are needed they should be completed within 12 hours of the injury.
- If wound does not appear better in 48 hours (improved colour or scab forming), see your family doctor.
- Puncture wounds (for example, from a nail, animal or human tooth) are much more likely to become infected. Watch for infection.
- If bandage sticks to the wound, try soaking it off in warm water.
- If finger is amputated, place it in a clean wet wash cloth and take it with you to the emergency department immediately.

CUTS & ABRASIONS

READ WARNING

FIRST AID

- Apply pressure to wound until bleeding stops.
- Clean well with mild soap and water after bleeding has stopped.
- Pat dry.

DO ANY OF THE FOLLOWING APPLY?

- Bleeding will not stop when pressure is applied continuously for 10 minutes.
- Cut is 1/2 in. (1 cm) or longer or on the face.
- Cut is deep (edges are gaping).
- Movement or feeling beyond cut is affected (see WARNING).

YES

NO

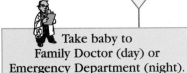 Take baby to
Family Doctor (day) or
Emergency Department (night).

TREATMENT

- Clean daily.
- Apply Topical Antibiotic to wound after cleaning.
- Cover to protect from contamination during the day.
- Check daily for infection (pain, pus, redness, or swelling).

Improvement in 48 hours?

YES

NO

Baby's Okay

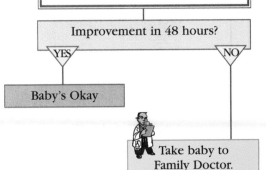 Take baby to
Family Doctor.

CUTS & ABRASIONS

CUTS & ABRASIONS

Trade Secrets

- The most important aspects of treating cuts and abrasions in children is to clean the wound thoroughly with soap and water to remove contamination and thereby prevent infection.
  Make sure that you wash your hands before washing your child's wound.
- Kissing a wound may cause infection.
  Teach your child that this is not to be done.
- Teach your child that scabs fall off on their own; they don't need help.
- Picking off scabs may cause infection or scars.
- Cuts or abrasions that don't heal within two weeks of injury should be seen by your family doctor.

Definitions

- **Abrasion** is a scraping off of the skin surface.
- **Cut** is an injury to the body causing a tearing or breaking of the skin surface.

Synonyms

- Scrape
- Skinned knee or elbow
- Laceration
- Tear
- Open wound
- Penetrating wound
- Puncture wound

Medications/Treatments

- **Acetaminophen Infant Drops** (e.g., Tempra, Tylenol) are used to both control pain and lower a fever. Do not use ASA or aspirin.
- **Antibiotic Ointments** (e.g., Bactroban, Baciguent, Polysporin) are used to prevent the wounds from getting infected.
- **Mild Soaps** (e.g., Johnson's Baby Body Wash, Baby Magic, Dove) are those that are gentle on a child's skin.

DIAPER RASH

Caroline was six months old when she was brought in to the office.

"She has had a terrible rash on her bottom for the past three days," her mother exclaimed. "It doesn't seem to bother her much, but it keeps getting worse. Her bowels are working normally, and I have changed diaper brands and tried various over-the-counter diaper creams, but nothing seems to be working."

On examination, Caroline was happy and healthy except for the bright red rash on the skin under her diaper. The rash also involved the skin folds in this area and was surrounded by red dots.

Caroline had thrush (yeast diaper rash) and needed a prescription cream to treat her first case of diaper rash.

Diaper rash is like an unwanted house guest:
after three days you may need help with the removal.

DIAPER RASH

DIAPER RASH

SYMPTOMS

- Rash (usually red) in diaper area

GOALS

Keep the area clean and dry to allow for natural healing.

TIPS

- Change wet and soiled diapers immediately (check every hour).
- Stop using all diaper wipes. Avoid alcohol for cleaning.
  Avoid plastic pants.
- Do not use talcum powder.
- Increase air exposure. For example, during naps place a non-plastic
  protective sheet under baby and remove diaper. Alternatively, attach
  diaper loosely at nap times to allow increased air flow.
- Clean baby's bottom with lukewarm water during each diaper change
  and pat dry. A cotton ball with mineral oil may also be used for cleaning.
  Apply a barrier cream with each diaper change.
- Try switching diaper type or brand if rashes keep occurring.
- The newer super-absorbent disposable diapers (e.g., Pampers, Huggies,
  Luvs) are extremely good at keeping baby's skin dryer.
- Some physicians recommend putting a couple of drops of baby oil in
  warm water in a spray bottle. Spray on the diaper area to clean and
  wipe off with a soft cloth. This may be less irritating than using water
  or wipes alone.
- Cloth diaper tips: Wash twice, the first time with detergent, and add
  a half a cup of vinegar to first rinse cycle. The second wash should be
  in half a cup of bleach to kill the germs left on the diapers.
  Change to milder detergent or fabric softener if rashes become recurrent.
  Hang diapers outside on the line to dry if possible.
- Do not use Vaseline or similar petroleum jellies to treat diaper rash.

DIAPER RASH

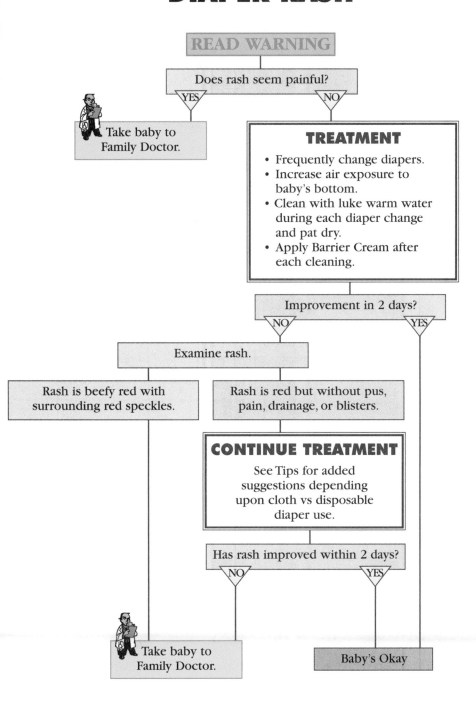

READ WARNING

Does rash seem painful?

YES → Take baby to Family Doctor.

NO →

TREATMENT
- Frequently change diapers.
- Increase air exposure to baby's bottom.
- Clean with luke warm water during each diaper change and pat dry.
- Apply Barrier Cream after each cleaning.

Improvement in 2 days?

NO → Examine rash.

YES →

Rash is beefy red with surrounding red speckles.

Rash is red but without pus, pain, drainage, or blisters.

CONTINUE TREATMENT
See Tips for added suggestions depending upon cloth vs disposable diaper use.

Has rash improved within 2 days?

NO → Take baby to Family Doctor.

YES → Baby's Okay

DIAPER RASH

DIAPER RASH

Trade Secrets

- Almost all babies will develop a diaper rash. It does not mean that you are a bad or negligent parent. They are most common when children start solid foods or while on antibiotics.
- The secret to treating diaper rash is to change and clean regularly, increase air exposure and create a barrier (with cream) between the diaper and baby's skin.
- Diaper rash is often associated with thrush; watch for it. (See Thrush, page 109).
- Irritant diaper rashes often progress into yeast diaper rashes after 2 days. The sooner you cure the rash the less likely it will get infected with yeast or bacteria.

Definitions

- **Air Exposure** is removing clothing (including diapers) to allow skin to air dry.
- **Blisters** are skin sores containing liquid, pus or blood.
- **Diaper Rash** includes a number of types of rashes that occur under the diaper in babies.
- **Diaper Wipes** include many commercial products for cleaning the diaper area that may also contain soaps, alcohol and /or perfumes that may irritate.
- **Talcum Powder** is a dusting powder that should *not* be used in baby care because of the risk of causing lung disease.

Synonyms

- Atopic dermatitis
- Candidiasis
- Contact dermatitis
- Diaper dermatitis
- Fungal dermatitis
- Irritant dermatitis
- Monilial dermatitis
- Seborrheic dermatitis
- Yeast dermatitis

Medications/Treatments

- **Barrier Creams** (e.g., Zincofax, Ihles Paste, Penetin) are zinc-based creams used to protect the skin from causes of irritation.
- **Mild Soaps** (e.g., Johnson's Baby Body Wash, Baby Magic, Dove) are those that are the most gentle on a baby's skin.
- **Mineral Oil** often helps in both cleaning and lubricating irritated skin.

DIAPER RASH

DIARRHEA

Angela was 18 months when she was brought to the office.

"She has had diarrhea for the last two days," her mother said. "She isn't eating very well, but she is still drinking a fair bit. Angela has had a fever of 38.5°C (101.3°F) off and on. She also seems to be in pain just prior to her episodes of diarrhea and has been having a watery poop at least six times a day."

Examination showed a happy and healthy girl with no evidence of dehydration or any skin rashes.

Angela had diarrhea.

A child with diarrhea is like a man crawling through the desert: if you don't replace the fluid losses, it is only a matter of time before he becomes dehydrated.

DIARRHEA

DIARRHEA

SYMPTOMS

• Frequent or mushy, loose, watery bowel movements

GOALS

Prevent dehydration until diarrhea resolves.

TIPS

- For the first six hours offer a tablespoon of oral replacement solution (e.g., Pedialyte, Lytren, Gastrolyte) every 15 minutes. If baby vomits, wait one hour then start again. If no vomiting after the first hour try 2 tablespoons every 15 minutes.
- Oral replacement solutions are made especially for children with vomiting or diarrhea. Do not use sugary drinks such as soda pop, fruit drinks, juice, sweet tea, etc.
- After six hours you may try the following if the diarrhea is improving:
    - Try to restart regular formula, soy formula or whole milk.
    - Try a graduated age-appropriate diet.
    Example: **BRAT** diet (**B**ananas, **R**ice, **A**pple sauce, **T**oast).
    Cereal, crackers and pablum are also okay if age-appropriate.
- For babies on formula or whole milk, continue using clear fluids until diarrhea is improving. *Use clear fluids only* for a maximum of 24 hrs.
- Most children may resume their regular diet after 24 hours.
- Odor and colour of the bowel movement is important.
  The greener and smellier the stool, the more severe the infection.
- Change diapers frequently. Clean buttocks with a mild soap and water, then pat dry. Apply a barrier cream after each washing.
- Wash your hands well after each change to avoid infecting others.

DIARRHEA

DIARRHEA

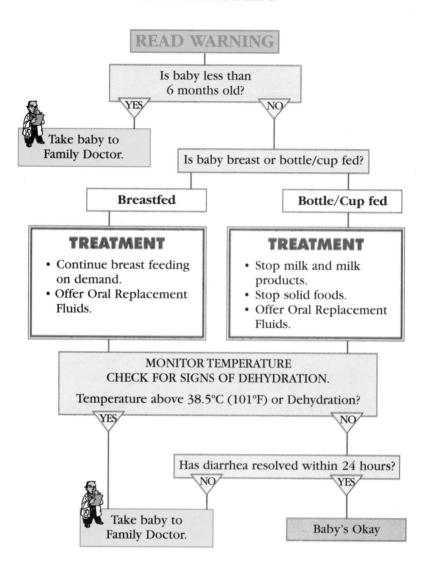

READ WARNING

Is baby less than 6 months old?

YES → Take baby to Family Doctor.

NO → Is baby breast or bottle/cup fed?

Breastfed

TREATMENT
- Continue breast feeding on demand.
- Offer Oral Replacement Fluids.

Bottle/Cup fed

TREATMENT
- Stop milk and milk products.
- Stop solid foods.
- Offer Oral Replacement Fluids.

MONITOR TEMPERATURE
CHECK FOR SIGNS OF DEHYDRATION.

Temperature above 38.5°C (101°F) or Dehydration?

YES → Take baby to Family Doctor.

NO → Has diarrhea resolved within 24 hours?

NO → Take baby to Family Doctor.

YES → Baby's Okay

SIGNS OF DEHYDRATION
• Dry mouth and tongue • Cracked lips • No tears • Sunken eyes
• No urine in 6 hours (or less than 6 diapers per day)
• Depressed soft spot on scalp • Lethargic

FLUIDS TO USE IN INFANTS
Oral Replacement Solutions are made especially for
children with vomiting or diarrhea

FLUIDS TO AVOID IN INFANTS
Sugary drinks such as:
soda pop, fruit drinks, juice, sweat tea, etc.

DIARRHEA

DIARRHEA

Trade Secrets

- Drink, drink, drink. Diarrhea in children can quickly lead to dehydration, especially if associated with vomiting or other symptoms of illness.
- Most physicians will recommend seeing an infant with diarrhea every 24 to 48 hours during an illness to check their hydration.
- Most children with an acute diarrhea illness are better within a week.
- When vomiting and diarrhea occur together, treat the vomiting first.
- The most common cause of diarrhea in this age group is rotavirus, with its peak incidence in the winter months.

Definitions

- **Bowel Movement** is stool or feces.
- **Breastfeeding on Demand** is breastfeeding when baby seems hungry.
- **Dehydration** is the loss of too much body water.
- **Diarrhea** is the frequent passage of watery stools.
- **Electrolytes** are certain chemicals – including sodium, potassium, chloride and bicarbonate – found in the tissues and blood. They are often measured as an aid to patient care.
- **Graduated Diet** means to start with what baby can tolerate and progress to what is needed (their normal healthy diet).

Synonyms

- Gastroenteritis
- The flu
- "Gastro"
- Travellers diarrhea (Montezumas Revenge, Bali Belly)
- The trots

Medications/Treatments

- **Barrier Creams** (e.g., Zincofax, Ihles Paste, Penetin) are zinc-based creams used to protect the skin from causes of irritation.
- **Mild Soaps** (e.g., Johnson's Baby Body Wash, Baby Magic, Dove) are those that are gentle on a baby's skin.
- **Oral Replacement Solutions** (e.g., Gastrolyte, Lytren, Pedialyte) are medicines that should be used to replace the fluid and electrolyte losses in children with vomiting or diarrhea.

DIARRHEA

EAR ACHES

Sylvia was nine months old when she was brought in to the office.

"Sylvia was up all last night," reported her exhausted mother. "If I held her up and rocked her, she would fall asleep, but every time that I went to lay her down she would wake up and start crying again. She also felt hot last night but I couldn't tell if it was from a fever or the relentless crying since I couldn't find my thermometer. She has had a bit of a cold with a slight fever for the past two days, but had been playing, eating and happy up until just last night."

Examination revealed a tired baby girl who was just finishing up an upper respiratory infection (cold). A look into her ear canals showed the cause of the problem.

Sylvia had her first ear infection.

There are very few things that will wake an otherwise healthy baby out of a sound sleep, so if laying your baby down is getting you up, think ear infection.

EAR ACHES

EAR ACHES

SYMPTOMS

- Pulling at or rubbing an ear • Awakens crying
- Uncontrollable crying • Irritability

GOALS

Control pain until seen by a doctor for antibiotics and analgesics (pain killers).

TIPS

- More than half of all children will get an ear infection.
- Few things will waken an infant from a sound sleep.
  If this happens, an ear ache is a possible cause.
- Raising the head of your baby's bed 5–10 centimeters (2–4 inches)
  may give some pain relief.
- Give acetaminophen infant drops every four hours while
  your baby is awake to help control the pain and fever.
- Analgesic ear drops and warm water bottle on the outer ear
  may help relieve pain. Be careful not to burn the ear.
  Use ear drops only on the advice of your doctor.
- Avoid flying with a baby who has an ear infection.
- Ear aches frequently follow colds or the flu. Watch for them.
- Always have the ear rechecked by your family doctor after an antibiotic
  treatment is completed. This will help prevent recurrent episodes.
- Do not allow your child to self-feed formula while lying on their back.
- Finish all of the antibiotic prescribed for your baby's ear infection.
  If you stop giving the antibiotic before it's all gone, the infection may
  return and this promotes the development of antibiotic-resistant bacteria.
- Ear aches that continue after two to three days of antibiotic treatment
  should be rechecked by your family doctor.
- Recurrent ear infections (usually more than six per year)
  will likely need a visit to the ear, nose and throat (ENT) specialist.

EAR ACHES

Is it Day or Night?

DAY TREATMENT

- Check temperature.
- Give acetaminophen (infant drops) as directed for pain & fever.
- Try decongestant infant drops.

NIGHT TREATMENT

- Check temperature.
- Give acetaminophen (infant drops) as directed for pain & fever.
- Try decongestant infant drops.
- Elevate head of bed 5 - 10 cm (2 - 4 inches)

Do symptoms improve?

YES   NO

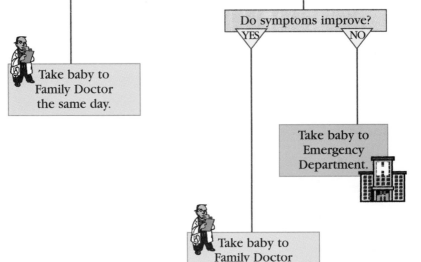

Take baby to Family Doctor the same day.

Take baby to Emergency Department.

Take baby to Family Doctor the following day.

EAR ACHES

Trade Secrets

- Almost all children develop ear infections in the preschool years. The peak incidence seems to be between six months and three years. There is often a family history of ear infections.
- To help prevent ear infections, do not allow smoking in the house, and make sure you feed your baby in an upright position, not while baby is lying down.
- Breast feed your baby and try to avoid sending your child to daycare.

Definitions

- **Ear Ache** refers to any pain in the ear.
- **Middle Ear Infection** (otitis media) refers to an infection behind the eardrum.
- **Outer Ear Infection** (swimmer's ear) refers to an infection in the ear canal.

Synonyms

- Acute otitis media
- Inner ear infection
- Middle ear infection
- Otitis media
- Serous otitis media

Medications/Treatments

- **Acetaminophen Infant Drops** (e.g., Tempra, Tylenol) are used to control pain and lower fever. Do not use ASA or aspirin.
- **Analgesic Ear Drops** or **Warmed Mineral Oil** (talk with your doctor) are often used to help relieve pain. Warm them to body temperature first. Do not use any drops if there is any drainage from the ear canal.
- **Antibiotics** (see your doctor), such as penicillin and amoxicillin, are used to treat bacterial ear infections. As more than 70 percent of ear infections are thought to be viral, your doctor may initially choose not to start your child on antibiotics.
- **Decongestants or Antihistamine-Decongestants** (e.g., Dimetapp oral infant drops, Triaminic oral infant drops) are used to relieve nasal and sinus congestion and postnasal drip. Do not administer decongestants or antihistamines in children less than 6 months old without first consulting your family doctor.
- **Ventilation Tubes** are used to drain the middle ear.

EAR ACHES

EYE INFECTIONS

Amanda was 15 months old when she was brought in to the office.

"Amanda has been getting green pus in her eyes for the past two days," her mother stated. "She is just finishing a cold and her older brother Bart, who is in kindergarten, brought home pink eye last week. In the mornings it is the worst; her eyes are usually stuck shut with a yellow-green crust. I have to use a warm wash cloth to remove the crusts so she can open her eyes."

On examination, Amanda had yellow-green crusts in the lashes and around her eyes. The whites of her eyes were slightly red. Amanda's eyes were itchy, as she was rubbing them constantly.

Amanda had pink eye (conjunctivitis).

Pink eye is like an Australian bush fire:
just when you think you have extinguished the problem in
one area/family member it erupts in another.

EYE INFECTIONS

EYE INFECTIONS

SYMPTOMS

- Discharge of pus • Eye stuck shut after sleep
- Excessive tearing, itching or burning • Bloodshot eyes • Sensitivity to light

GOALS

Keep baby's eye clean until the antibiotics can correct the infection.
Prevent the infection from spreading to other family members.

TIPS

- Eye infections are very contagious. Use a separate wash cloth and towel for baby. Wash your hands thoroughly after cleaning or treating the eye.
- Wipe sticky eyelids with a warm moist wash cloth as needed. Use a fresh cloth for each eye.
- Use only antibiotic drops prescribed by your family doctor for this problem. Do not reuse drops without your doctor's okay.
- Apply drops by gently pulling down the lower eye lid and placing the drops inside the lower lid.
- Often two people are needed to place drops in a baby's eye.
- Eye drops are most easily applied when your baby is feeding.
- See doctor again if antibiotic drops do not clear the eye within 72 hrs.
- Other than infection, common causes of pink eye include irritants such as tobacco smoke, dust, smog, shampoo or chlorinated swimming pool and tub water.
- Avoid eye irritants such as tobacco smoke, dust or bright sunlight while eye is healing.
- Eye ointment may be better in children under one year, as it stays in the eye longer so infections may heal faster. It is also easier to apply. Lay the ointment along the eye lid (over the lashes) and the child will blink it in.
- Blocked tear ducts are a common cause of tearing in babies. This usually starts about week two and may last for up to one year. See your family doctor for advice on how to look after this condition.

EYE INFECTIONS

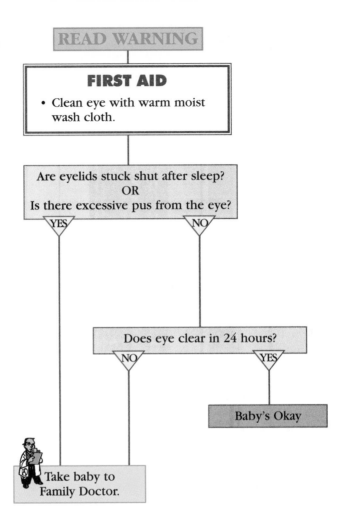

READ WARNING

FIRST AID

- Clean eye with warm moist wash cloth.

Are eyelids stuck shut after sleep?
OR
Is there excessive pus from the eye?

YES   NO

Does eye clear in 24 hours?

NO   YES

Baby's Okay

Take baby to Family Doctor.

COMMON CAUSES
OF PINK EYE

- Eye infection
- Eye allergy
- Eye irritant
- Eye abrasion
- Blocked tear duct

EYE INFECTIONS

Trade Secrets

- Eye infections can be very contagious. This is why it is so important to follow your doctor's advice, and to continue antibiotic eye drop treatment for at least 2 days after the eye appears to be back to normal.
- One of the most difficult things to do is put drops into the eyes of children. It is best to use two people for this. The "one person" hold is difficult but possible with the child face up with their head between your knees and their arms under your knees while you are in a sitting position.
- Some parents find that they simply cannot get the child's eyelids open to put in the drops. In this case, when applying drops, simply place the drops in the inner corner of the eye. If applying ointment, place along the eye lid margin. In both cases, when the child eventually opens the eye the drops or ointment will enter the eye.

Definitions

- **Eye Infection** is an invasion of micro-organisms into the eye that causes infection.
- **Excessive Tearing** is a pronounced watering of the eyes.
- **Pink Eye** may be caused by a multitude of conditions: allergic, infective, chemical and irritative.
  (Eye infection is just one of the causes.)
- **Sensitivity to Light** is eye discomfort upon exposure to bright light.

Synonyms

- Conjunctivitis
- Pink eye
- Red eye

Medications/Treatments

- Can differ depending upon the cause of the eye infection.
- **Bacterial infections** are treated with various antibiotic eye drops.
- **Viral infections** are treated with antiviral eye drops.

FEBRILE SEIZURES

Ahmed was two years old when he was rushed to the emergency department.

"He has been running a high fever for the past couple of days, but today it wouldn't come down with Tylenol," his father gasped. "He suddenly just went limp, his eyes rolled back and he started twitching all over. He has had fevers in the past, but nothing like this."

Examination using an ear probe thermometer revealed a fever of 40°C (104°F). Ahmed had bitten his tongue and wet his diaper during the seizure, but now seemed comfortable, although drowsy. There were no signs of serious medical problems but he did have two severely infected tonsils. On further discussion with Ahmed's parents, I discovered that he had developed cold-like symptoms three days prior, and had been complaining of a sore throat (with decreased appetite) over the past 24 hours.

Ahmed had experienced his first febrile seizure.

Febrile seizures are a lot like winning a prize at the local fair:
it's unlikely but possible.

Watching your child have their first febrile seizure
is a parental cardiac stress test.

FEBRILE SEIZURES

FEBRILE SEIZURES

SYMPTOMS

• Eyes roll back • Body stiffens and /or twitches and shakes
• Child usually appears unconscious during the seizure

GOALS

Protect the baby during the seizure,
then lower the temperature after the seizure.

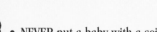

TIPS

- NEVER put a baby with a seizure in the bath tub.
- Protect baby's airway during the seizure. Keep it open and clear, especially if they vomit. Do not restrain any part of baby during the seizure, including their tongue. Don't force anything into baby's mouth.
- Protect them from any injury by cradling them in your arms or placing them on a bed or other location that is soft and padded.
  Place them in the side-sleeping recovery position in case they vomit.
- Most seizures only last for one to two minutes.
- Try to reduce the fever. You may use acetaminophen by mouth when baby is alert enough. Alternatively, use acetaminophen suppositories.
- Sponge baby with cool wet cloths to reduce fever.
- Most fever (febrile) seizures occur at temperatures above 40°C (104°F).
- Fever seizures do not cause brain damage.
- The secret to controlling and preventing seizures is to try to control the fever. Therefore, monitor and treat your baby's fever closely during periods of illness.
- See the Fever section (page 77) for tips on how to control a fever.
- Watch for fever following any immunization.
- Keep track of the number of seizures and their duration.
- Take your baby to your family doctor or the Emergency Department if your baby should have a seizure.

FEBRILE SEIZURES

SEIZURE TREATMENT

- Keep airway clear
  (remove food or vomit from mouth).
- Place infant in soft padded area
  and protect from injury.
- **DO NOT** put anything in baby's
  mouth during seizure.
- **DO NOT** give foods, fluids, or
  medicine during seizures.
- **DO NOT** put baby in bath tub
  during or after a seizure.

Use a clock to time length of seizure.

Does seizure last more than 5 minutes?

YES   NO

CALL 911
or
EMERGENCY
MEDICAL SERVICES

POST-SEIZURE TREATMENT

- Take temperature and give
  Acetaminophen Infant Drops
  when baby awakens or
  Acetaminophen suppositories
  while still asleep.
- Sponge with cool wet cloths.
- Give cool clear fluids to the child
  when they wake up,

Take baby to
Family Doctor (day) or
Emergency Department (night).

*Guidelines for performing
Cardio-Pulmonary Resuscitation (CPR)
are found on pages 120 to 126 of this book.*

Please get training in advance for infant/child CPR.

FEBRILE SEIZURES

FEBRILE SEIZURES

Trade Secrets

- About 2 to 5% of children experience a febrile seizure.
  Most outgrow them by six years of age.
  It seems that once a child's brain matures, the risk of seizure drops.
- A family history of febrile seizures increases the risk of a febrile seizure
  as well as the risk of recurrence.
- Most fever (febrile) seizures occur between the ages of six months
  and four years. The average age is about 18 months.
- About one-third of children with one febrile seizure will
  go on to have another, usually within two years.
- Febrile seizures do not cause learning problems, mental retardation,
  cerebral palsy, epilepsy, lower I.Q. scores, behavioral problems,
  development problems or death.
- Febrile seizures are difficult to predict and prevent.
- The higher the temperature attained during the first seizure the less
  chance of a febrile seizure recurrence.
- Approximately 4% of children who have febrile seizure will go on to
  have epilepsy. This means that 96% *will not* develop epilepsy.

Definitions

- **Febrile Seizures** are seizures caused by an elevation in body
  temperature. They generally result in a loss of consciousness and
  convulsions (violent shaking). Most commonly found in children.
- **Repetitive Seizures** are recurrent or repeating seizures.

Synonyms

- Febrile convulsions
- Febrile fits
- Fever epilepsy
- Fever seizure

Medications/Treatments

- **Acetaminophen Infant Drops** (e.g., Tempra, Tylenol)
  are used to control pain and lower fever. Do not use ASA or aspirin.
- **Acetaminophen Suppositories** are for the same purpose,
  but are placed in the rectum when treatment by mouth is undesirable.
- **Anticonvulsant or Anti-Seizure Medications**
  (e.g., Dilantin, Phenobarbital, Tegretol) are used to prevent seizures.
- **Anti-inflammatories** (e.g., childrens Motrin, Advil)) are used for pain
  and fever control.
- **Diazepam** (valium) is used to treat or prevent recurrent seizures.
- **Lumbar Puncture** is performed by placing a small needle on the back
  and is frequently performed in children under 2 years of age to rule out
  the possibility of meningitis (infection of the spinal cord).

FEVER

Jennifer was two years old when she was brought into the emergency department.

"She has been running a temperature for the past two days," her mother said. "Initially it seemed to go down with Tylenol but since last night that doesn't seem to be working anymore. She has been sleeping more in the last two days; she is not eating her solids but continues to drink fairly well. She has also had some cold-like symptoms for the past few days with a runny nose and a slight cough. My main concern is that she might get brain damage with this fever."

With further discussion I discovered that Jennifer's mom had been using the hand-on-forehead method of temperature-taking, and had not actually used a thermometer.

On examination, Jennifer showed symptoms of a cold. An ear probe thermometer revealed a temperature of 38.5°C (101.3°F).

Jennifer had a fever.

I explained to Jennifer's mother the relevance of fever as well as the importance of thermometers in the treatment of childhood illness. I also reviewed with her the appropriate dosage and timing of acetaminophen for Jennifer.

*Fever is much like the North American wolf:
surrounded by a lot of misunderstanding
and unfounded fear. As physicians, our job is to
clear up fever's bad reputation by educating people
on when and how best to treat it.*

FEVER

FEVER

WARNING

***Take baby to Family Doctor or Emergency Department
IMMEDIATELY if you see ANY of the following:***

- Temperature above 38.5°C (101.3°F) • Seizures • Uncontrolled crying
Vomiting • Ear pain or baby is rubbing ears • New rashes or bruises
  - Trouble breathing • Sore or stiff neck • Diarrhea
    - Drowsiness or irritability • Restlessness
- Fever related to heat / humidity exposure (heat exhaustion, heat stroke)
  - Your child looks or acts sick

NEVER give aspirin (ASA) to a baby with fever,
due to the risk of Reye's syndrome.

SYMPTOMS

- Skin feels warm and sweaty
- Face pinker than usual (flushed)

GOALS

Reduce fever. Keep comfortable. Prevent seizures.

TIPS

- Fever usually means your baby is fighting an infection.
- Normal temperature varies depending on where it is taken.
The following are considered normal:
  - Under arm (36.4°C or 97.6°F)
  - In mouth (37°C or 98.6°F)
  - Rectal (37.6°C or 99.6°F).
- Fever below 39.5°C (103.1°F) is not normally harmful.
- Seizures may occur with temperatures greater than 40°C (104°F),
or with a rapid rise in temperature. In a seizure the baby's entire body
suddenly stiffens, then shakes. Follow the Febrile Seizures flow chart
on page 75.
- Keep baby lightly and loosely dressed in cotton for comfort.
- Keep baby's room cool, but avoid cold drafts and breezes.
- Encourage increased fluids (water, juice or fruit juice popsicles).
- Use acetaminophen in correct dosage to treat fever.
- Continue to feed your baby as normal. Use nutritious favorite foods.
- Try to keep a child with fever calm. Overexertion may cause higher
temperatures.
- Sponge baby with lukewarm (never hot) water. NEVER put a baby with
seizures in a bath. NEVER use alcohol on baby's skin or in the bath.
- NEVER give a cold water enema to a child with fever.

FEVER

FEVER

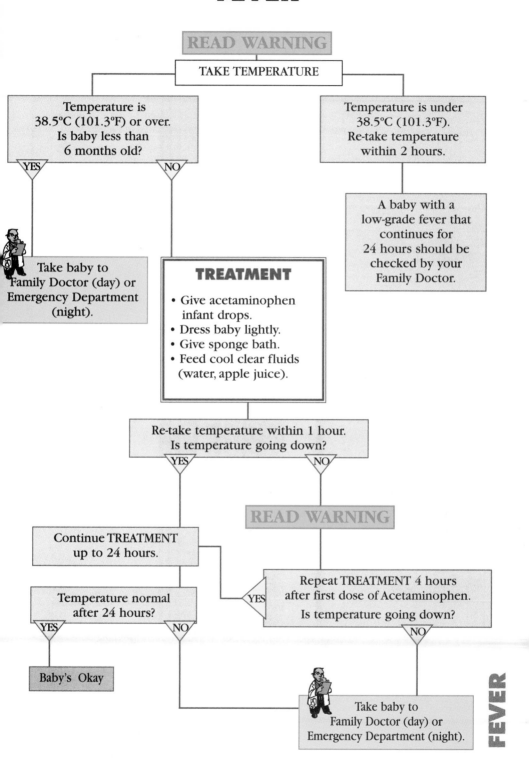

TAKE TEMPERATURE

Temperature is 38.5°C (101.3°F) or over. Is baby less than 6 months old?

YES — Take baby to Family Doctor (day) or Emergency Department (night).

NO

Temperature is under 38.5°C (101.3°F). Re-take temperature within 2 hours.

A baby with a low-grade fever that continues for 24 hours should be checked by your Family Doctor.

TREATMENT

- Give acetaminophen infant drops.
- Dress baby lightly.
- Give sponge bath.
- Feed cool clear fluids (water, apple juice).

Re-take temperature within 1 hour. Is temperature going down?

YES / NO

Continue TREATMENT up to 24 hours.

READ WARNING

Temperature normal after 24 hours?

YES — Baby's Okay

NO

Repeat TREATMENT 4 hours after first dose of Acetaminophen. Is temperature going down?

YES

NO — Take baby to Family Doctor (day) or Emergency Department (night).

FEVER

FEVER

Trade Secrets

- The secret to curing a fever is uncovering the cause.
- Treat fever to make the child feel more comfortable and to reduce high temperatures, thereby preventing febrile or fever seizures.
- Use the "take temperature, treat temperature, take temperature" approach; this way you can determine whether your fever-reducing approach is working.
- Do not expect sponge baths or acetaminophen to bring the temperature back to normal. It may bring the temperature down about 1°C (2°F).
- Children with fevers should be kept away from others until the fever has been gone for 24 hours. This includes daycare, sitters and play groups.

Definitions

- **Fever** is a sign that the body has developed an infection.
  By raising the temperature, the body may be able to cure infections more quickly.
- **Reye's Syndrome** is a rare condition with brain and liver damage and a mortality (death) rate of greater than 40 percent.
  It may be associated with consumption of ASA-containing products during a viral infection.
- **Seizures** result in loss of consciousness and convulsions (violent shaking).
- **Uncontrolled Crying** is prolonged crying lasting longer than 2 hours.

Synonyms

- Febrile illness
- High body temperature
- Pyrexia

Medications/Treatments

- **Acetaminophen Infant Drops** (e.g., Tempra, Tylenol) are used to both control pain and lower fever.
  Do not use ASA or aspirin.
- **Acetaminophen Suppositories** are placed in the rectum to reduce pain and fever.
- **Cool compresses and baths** help cool the child but often cause shivering.

CASE STUDY

Colin was 14 months old when he was brought in to the office.

"He was running with his brother when he slipped and fell," his mother announced. "He hit his head on the coffee table. I don't think that he was knocked out as he cried right away. I'm especially concerned because he vomited once after the fall. I'm not sure whether it was due to the fall or because he was crying so hard after the accident. Now he seems so drowsy. I've done my best but I'm having a hard time keeping him awake."

Examination of Colin revealed a healthy but tired boy. His neurologic examination was normal. There was no cut to the skin, but he was developing a large bruise (goose egg) on his forehead. His mother assured me that she had seen no change in his walking or talking since the accident.

This was to be the first of many head injuries for rambunctious Colin over the next several years. His mother became very adept with the head injury routine.

Head injuries and kids go together like dogs and fleas.

The vigilance of the observing parent should match or exceed the force of the blow causing the head injury (i.e., the harder the hit the closer you watch).

HEAD INJURIES

SYMPTOMS

- History of hitting the head or crying while holding the head
- Skin may be scraped, cut, bruised or swollen
- The scalp has an excellent blood supply so cuts may bleed profusely

GOALS

Treat the injury and observe for complications.

TIPS

- Allow the child to rest or sleep after the injury.
  Keeping them awake is not as important as observing and waking
  (wake / check every two hours during the day and every two to four
  hours at night looking for warning symptoms).
- Vomiting once or twice is common after a head injury but repeated
  vomiting is not.
- Feed your child only clear fluids for two to four hours after
  a head injury.
- Apply pressure to any bleeding wound and ice and pressure to any bruise
  or swelling. Wash all scrapes and abrasions with mild soap and water.
  Wounds bleeding after 10 minutes of pressure may need stitches.
- Monitor baby's symptoms for 24 to 48 hours after a head injury.
  A child may return to normal activities after 48 hours if they are
  without symptoms of a more severe injury.
- Do not use a pain killer stronger than acetaminophen without your
  doctor's advice. Do not use aspirin after a head injury, as it may
  increase the possibility of bleeding.
- Younger children (less than one year) usually need to be seen by
  a doctor because it can be difficult to evaluate their symptoms.

HEAD INJURIES

HEAD INJURIES

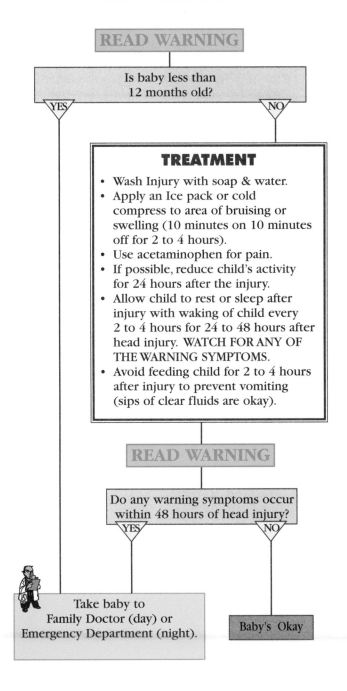

READ WARNING

Is baby less than
12 months old?

YES   NO

TREATMENT

- Wash Injury with soap & water.
- Apply an Ice pack or cold compress to area of bruising or swelling (10 minutes on 10 minutes off for 2 to 4 hours).
- Use acetaminophen for pain.
- If possible, reduce child's activity for 24 hours after the injury.
- Allow child to rest or sleep after injury with waking of child every 2 to 4 hours for 24 to 48 hours after head injury. WATCH FOR ANY OF THE WARNING SYMPTOMS.
- Avoid feeding child for 2 to 4 hours after injury to prevent vomiting (sips of clear fluids are okay).

READ WARNING

Do any warning symptoms occur
within 48 hours of head injury?

YES   NO

Take baby to
Family Doctor (day) or
Emergency Department (night).

Baby's Okay

Head Injuries

HEAD INJURIES

Trade Secrets

- Checking pupils is difficult for parents and often unreliable.
  It is often best saved for the hospital staff trained in this evaluation tool.
- Head injuries are extremely common among babies, especially when
  learning to walk. Learn how to evaluate and treat them.
- Children may be admitted to hospital if the head injury has been
  severe or if a child has vomited three or more times, or
  had a period of unconsciousness lasting five or more minutes.
- Observation of a child after a head injury is most important in the first
  12 hours. This is when you will generally see any serious symptoms.
  However, you must continue to observe the child for at least 24–48
  hours following any head injury.
- See "Childproofing"(page 127) to help prevent head injuries.
- Always use an approved infant car seat.
- The use of acetaminophen is controversial.
  Some physicians encourage bringing a child in for assessment if the
  head injury is severe enough to require analgesics (pain killers).
  Other physicians feel that treating the pain will help baby settle faster.

Definitions

- **Head Injury** is any traumatic wound to the head.
- **Concussion** is an injury to the brain due to a traumatic event
  (e.g., fall, blow).

Synonyms

- Brain bruise
- Cerebral contusion
- Cerebral hematoma
- Concussion

Medications/Treatments

- **Acetaminophen Infant Drops** (e.g., Tempra, Tylenol)
  are used to treat pain associated with head injuries.
  Do not use ASA or aspirin.
- **Ice Packs or Cold Compresses**
  (e.g., gel packs or a bag of frozen peas wrapped in a towel)
  can help to reduce swelling, bruising and pain at the injury site.

IMMUNIZATION REACTIONS

CASE STUDY

Gordon was two months old when he was brought in to the office.

"Two days ago he had his two-month needle and he has been miserable ever since," his mother explained. "He has been extremely irritable, has gone off his food, has a slight fever and seems to be in pain. Today I noticed a lump in his leg. That's when I thought I had better rush him in."

Examination revealed a healthy boy, except for a sore lump on his left leg as a result of his immunization injection of two days earlier. His temperature was 37.5°C (99.5°F).

Gordon had developed a local immunization reaction.

"Quote"

The pain of immunization reactions is a lot like the pain we receive from politicians: it may come from either a municipal (local) level or a national (general) level. Unfortunately, it frequently develops from both.

IMMUNIZATION REACTIONS

WARNING

Take baby to Family Doctor or Emergency Department IMMEDIATELY if you see ANY of the following:

- Fever of 39.5°C (103.1°F) or greater • Crying for more than three hours
- Seizures • Stiff neck • Drowsiness • Pale or blue skin
- Allergic reactions
(hives, wheezing, trouble breathing, swelling of face or mouth)
- Changes in behavior • Baby looks or acts sick

Infants with previous convulsions (febrile or non-febrile) are more likely to have seizures following the Pertussis vaccination.

SYMPTOMS

- Reactions to immunizations (booster shots) may be local or general

GOALS

To recognize reactions and treat symptoms.

TIPS

- Most children have little or no reaction to routine immunizations.
- Give acetaminophen infant drops just before an immunization injection and regularly as directed for the first 24 hours after the injection, especially if a child has a history of febrile seizures.
  Notify your doctor before immunization of any problems with previous immunizations.
- Apply a cold cloth to injection site as needed for pain relief.
- As with any medication, vaccination may cause side effects.
  Learn to recognize the symptoms if faced with an irritable child after immunization.
- If your baby is allergic to eggs, check first with your doctor before vaccination is done.
- For normal healthy children, the benefits of immunization far outweigh any possible side effects.
- Influenza vaccine is useful in preventing the three most serious, predicted influenza illnesses of that year. It will not prevent all 'flus'. It is generally given to children with other medical problems (such as heart disease, lung disease or chronic illness).

A chicken pox vaccine is available in the U.S. & Canada
The local and general reactions are similar to
DPT Polio Adsorbed.
The reactions can occur for up to one month after immunization.

IMMUNIZATION REACTIONS

Diphtheria, Pertussis, Tetanus, Polio (DPT Polio Adsorbed)
Side effects occur within 1 or 2 days of injection

LOCAL REACTION

- Mild Pain.
- Swelling.
- Redness.
- Lump at needle site.

GENERAL REACTION

- Fever.
- Decreased appetite.
- Irritable (fussy) often for 3 to 4 days after needle.
- Vomiting.

Hemophilus Influenza B (HIB)
Adverse effects are rare

LOCAL REACTION

- Mild Pain.
- Swelling.
- Redness.
- Lump at needle site.

GENERAL REACTION

- Mild Fever.
- Decreased appetite.
- Irritable (fussy).
- Diarrhea and/or Vomiting.
- Rash.

Measles, Mumps, Rubella (MMR)
Side effects occur within 1 or 2 weeks of injection

LOCAL REACTION

- Mild Pain.
- Swelling.
- Redness.
- Lump at needle site.

GENERAL REACTION

- Fever.
- Neck gland swelling.
- Rash 6 to 10 days after injection.
- Aching or swollen joints.
- Testicular swelling.

IMMUNIZATION REACTIONS

IMMUNIZATION REACTIONS

Trade Secrets

- Report all previous problems, including either local or general reactions to previous vaccinations, to your physician before they give the next inoculation.
- The incidence of reactions is very low. Most children can be vaccinated.
- Tell your physician of any illness or fever within the last few days preceding the vaccination.
- A child's attitude, activity level and appetite may be affected for one to two days following immunizations.
- Keep a copy of your child's vaccination record with other important household documents. Keep an extra copy with you.
- Children with a severe reaction to eggs may receive all vaccinations except measles and mumps, as these are grown in chick cell cultures. Many egg allergic children will tolerate measles and mumps vaccinations. An allergy consultation is recommended first, and special precautions must be taken before these children receive measles and mumps vaccines.

Definitions

- **General Reactions** refers to reactions that occur to the body as a whole.
- **Immunization Reactions** are unwanted side effects of a vaccination.
- **Local Reactions** refers to reactions that are at the site of the injection.

Synonyms

- Boosters
- Inoculations
- Vaccinations

Medications/Treatments

- **Acetaminophen Infant Drops** (e.g., Tempra Tylenol) are used to both control pain and lower fever. *Do not use ASA or aspirin.*
- **Cold Compresses or Ice Packs** (e.g., gel packs or a bag of frozen peas wrapped in a towel) are used to reduce swelling, redness and pain at the site of the inoculation.

JAUNDICE

CASE STUDY

Jasmine was 10 days old when she was brought in to the office.

"She seems to be getting yellow," her mother exclaimed. "She started three or four days after she was born, but now it seems to be getting worse. My sister told me that it was because I was breast feeding and that I should switch over to bottle feeding. What do you think?"

Jasmine's mom described a normal, full-term pregnancy and delivery.

On examination, Jasmine was indeed yellow (jaundiced) but was an otherwise healthy, alert and robust newborn. She was growing and developing normally.

"Quote"

A jaundiced baby is like hearing
your dog barking in the backyard:
both require some investigation into
the cause of the problem.

JAUNDICE

SYMPTOMS

- Yellow to orange colour, especially noticeable in the whites of the eyes and
  on the face, chest and stomach • Jaundiced babies often seem sleepy

GOALS

Rule out serious causes and treat regular causes of jaundice.

TIPS

- All babies suspected of jaundice should be seen by a doctor.
- Most jaundice in a healthy newborn is not serious and clears up
  easily and quickly.
- One of the best ways to assess jaundice is to place your baby, unclothed,
  in natural light or under fluorescent lights.
  Look for yellowness of the skin and whites of the eyes.
  You can also assess for jaundice by gently pressing on the tip of
  your baby's nose. Even in children of colour the skin will appear
  white if normal and yellow if jaundiced.
- Increase the frequency of feedings (breast or bottle) to at least every two
  hours.
- Ensure an adequate nipple latch and that baby is getting enough.
  Do not limit feeds. Do not stop breast feeding without your doctor's
  advice.
- Increasing fluid intake is not as important as having baby eat and
  therefore stool more frequently. Bilirubin (a jaundice-causing
  substance) is removed from the body in the stool, not in the urine.
- Jaundiced babies may be sleepy. Try waking and keeping baby awake by
  changing the diaper, removing some of their clothes, or stroking them
  under the chin while feeding. The more baby is awake and eating,
  the more quickly the jaundice will clear up.
- For mild cases of jaundice, place baby in a safe position in front of
  a window for an hour or so per day. Watch that baby is comfortable
  and doesn't overheat or get cold. Do not place baby in direct sunlight.

JAUNDICE

JAUNDICE

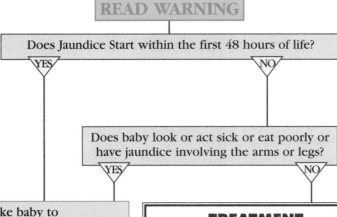

Does Jaundice Start within the first 48 hours of life?

YES — NO

Does baby look or act sick or eat poorly or have jaundice involving the arms or legs?

YES — NO

Take baby to
Family Doctor (day)
or Emergency Department (night)
or Notify the Nurse
if still in Hospital.

TREATMENT

- Increase frequency of breast or bottle feedings.
  Try to feed at least every 2 hours.
- Encourage baby to stay awake for the whole feeding.
  Stroke under their chin during feeding.
- Ensure an adequate nipple latch and that baby is getting enough (do a daily weight with baby).
- Do not limit feedings.
- Place baby in indirect sunlight.
- Watch for signs of dehydration.
- See Trade Secrets (pg. 92)

Does jaundice improve?

YES — NO

Baby's Okay

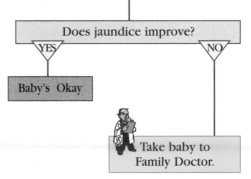

Take baby to
Family Doctor.

JAUNDICE

Trade Secrets

- Jaundice appears in over half of all full-term infants.
- Jaundice appears in over three-quarters of all premature infants.
- The more bowel movements the baby has per day, the sooner the bilirubin is cleared from the body, and the sooner the jaundice improves.
- Most babies produce two to three bowel movements (stools) per day by the third day of life. Black or green stool is normal for the first few days, then it usually turns yellow.
- Jaundice is not usually a danger as long as the bilirubin level is kept under certain limits. Ask your doctor for the upper limits of normal levels. blood tests help determine the bilirubin level.
- Most full-term babies will return to their birth weight by 2 weeks of age.
- Watch for signs of dehydration and inadequate milk intake:
  - fewer than six wet diapers per day or no urine in six hours
  - dry mouth and tongue
  - cracked lips
  - sunken eyes
  - depressed soft spot on top of the scalp (top of the head)
  - difficult to wake baby (excessively sleepy)

Definitions

- **Bilirubin** is a substance in the blood created from the breakdown of red blood cells. Jaundice is a condition caused by too much bilirubin in the body, making the skin look yellow. Jaundice can be dangerous if the bilirubin blood level becomes too high.
- **Physiologic (Normal) Jaundice** usually starts between two and four days old, and is gone by day 14.
- **Breast Milk Associated Jaundice** usually starts between four and seven days old and may last up to 12 weeks.
- **Stooling** is also known as having bowel movements (poop).

Synonyms

- Yellow jaundice

Medications/Treatments

- **High bilirubin** levels (jaundice) may require that the baby is treated with special lights (phototherapy) available in most hospitals.

NOSE BLEEDS

Bryan was two years old when he was brought in to the office one October morning.

"He keeps getting nose bleeds," his father explained. "He has had three in the past two weeks, and this morning he had some dried blood on his pillow. It hasn't slowed him down; in fact, I have a hard time keeping him still long enough to stop the bleeding."

Examination revealed a happy, busy boy without evidence of illness. Within his nose were some crusted, bloody scabs that Bryan had a hard time not picking. From his father we also discovered that there was no humidification in the house and their forced-air furnace had just started to run regularly. Others in the house had developed nose bleeds as well.

Bryan had nose bleeds caused by his low-humidity environment.

Advice was given on the correct technique to stop a nose bleed as well as general tips and treatment.

Stopping a nose bleed is like mastering sex: technique is everything.

Canadian winters have the same effect on skin and mucous membranes as they have on the paint of a weather-beaten barn door: it dries, cracks and flakes.

NOSE BLEEDS

NOSE BLEEDS

SYMPTOMS

- Hemorrhaging or blood loss through the nose.

GOALS

Stop the bleeding, allow time for healing and avoid further episodes.

TIPS

- Nose bleeds are usually one-sided and caused by colds, allergies, nose picking, dryness or cold weather.
- Keep baby upright (NOT lying down) and leaning forward, not back.
- Crying increases blood flow and therefore bleeding.
  Try to keep baby calm.
- Apply petroleum jelly to nasal passages (centre wall or septum) morning and night to protect blood vessels and allow for healing.
- Avoid blowing nose or sneezing after bleeding stops.
  This is obviously difficult to do with young infants.
- Try to stop child from picking their nose.
  Cut fingernails regularly to reduce the damage from nose picking sessions.
- Do not stuff anything into the nose to stop or prevent bleeding.
- Avoid using drying agents (such as decongestants or nasal sprays) or aspirin after a nose bleed.
- Use a vaporizer / humidifier in the bedroom at night and during naps.
- Help child with quiet activities after a nose bleed to reduce the chance of a recurrence.
- Elevate the head of the bed.
- treat allergies to reduce nose bleeds.
- Treat allergy symptoms using Allergic Reactions section (page 17).
- Stay calm! If you remain calm, so will your child.

NOSE BLEEDS

FIRST AID

- Have baby sit upright.
- Tilt head forward, not back.
- Pinch the soft part of nose between your thumb and forefinger.
  Time 5 minutes, using a clock.
- Try to keep your baby calm.

Does bleeding stop?

YES   NO

FOLLOW-UP

- Apply cold pack or ice to bridge of nose.
- Pinch nose as a First Aid for another 5 minutes.

Does bleeding stop?

YES   NO

HEALING TREATMENT

- Apply petroleum jelly (see Tips).
- Avoid pinching, blowing, cleaning or sneezing through nose for at least 24 hours.
- Keep baby quiet for 6 to 8 hours.

Take baby to Family Doctor (day) or Emergency Department (night).

Does bleeding re-start?

YES   NO

Re-start Flow Chart.

Baby's Okay

NOSE BLEEDS

NOSE BLEEDS

Trade Secrets

- Nose bleeds in children are usually a result of an injury (picking, falls or foreign objects) or inflammation (colds or allergies).
- Nose bleeds are common because of the rich blood supply in the nose. The blood vessels are covered with a very thin protective layer, and when this dries out, the bleeding begins.
- Proper pinching technique is vital to stop a nose bleed.
    - Make sure child is sitting up with head tilted forward, not back.
    - Make sure that you pinch the soft, not the hard, part of the nose.
- Cold packs to the back of the neck or the forehead are not helpful.
- Most nose bleeds will stop with first aid treatment.
- Nose bleeds are most common in winter months.
- Nose bleeds are most common in children aged 2 to 10.
- Prevention techniques:
    - Humidify the house, especially where your child sleeps.
    - Cut fingernails weekly to keep them short.
    - Use saline nose sprays to lubricate nasal passages.
    - Use petroleum jelly twice a day.

Definitions

- **Humidification** means to add moisture or humidity to the air we breath. This includes stand alone humidifiers, vaporizers or humidifiers that attach directly to the furnace.

Synonyms

- Bloody nose
- Epistaxis
- Nose hemorrhage

Medications/Treatments

- **Vasoconstrictor Agents** (pediatric Otrivin, Neosynephrine) are used to squeeze blood vessels to reduce blood flow.
- **Cautery** (silver nitrate sticks) are used to seal the leaking blood vessels.
- **Nasal Packing** with petroleum jelly gauze, may be used at the hospital for severe bleeds.
- **Petroleum Jelly** is used to cover and protect fragile irritated blood vessels in the nose.

NOSE BLEEDS

STOMACH ACHES

CASE STUDY

Briar was six months old when she was brought in to the office.

"She has been crying off and on for the past two days," her father said. "She seems to be okay for a while, but then she will draw her legs up to her chest and shriek with pain. She is not eating as well as before and has been incredibly gassy lately. Last night she was up three times. I even checked for fever but her temperature was normal. The other thing I think might be of importance is that we have been trying her on cereals and fruits over the last two months and her bowel habits have definitely changed. Her stools used to be regular and mushy and have now become more irregular and hard, like little rabbit pellets."

In this case, examination revealed a happy, healthy but constipated girl, which was causing her stomach aches.

When diagnosing pain in children, especially before the child can speak, one must become a detective. Parental intuition and deductive reasoning are the hallmarks of success.

STOMACH ACHES

SYMPTOMS

- Abdominal pain • Crying • Drawing up knees to chest
- Excessive gas • Cramps • Irritability
- May have vomiting, diarrhea or constipation

GOALS

Reduce discomfort, treat associated symptoms (for example, diarrhea), and determine cause if possible.

TIPS

- There are many causes for stomach ache, including: overeating, gas, constipation, lead poisoning (rare), colic (if three months or younger), food intolerance, gastroenteritis (flu), urinary tract infection, strep throat.
- Comfort your baby while you watch for symptoms.
- When thirsty, give oral replacement solutions or very diluted clear fluids, for example one part apple juice mixed with three parts water.
- When giving fluids with vomiting or diarrhea, give 1 tablespoon every 15 minutes or so.
  If child vomits, wait one hour then try again.
- Have your child lie down to rest.
- For comfort, try acetaminophen infant drops, a warm water bottle wrapped in a towel and a stomach massage.
- Do not force a child to eat or drink. Do not give laxatives, suppositories or enemas unless directed to by your doctor.
- Constipation is often blamed but rarely causes pain in babies until they are started on solid foods or cow's milk, or when their formula changes.
- Milk allergies (lactose intolerance) may cause abdominal cramps and excessive gassiness in baby.

STOMACH ACHES

STOMACH ACHES

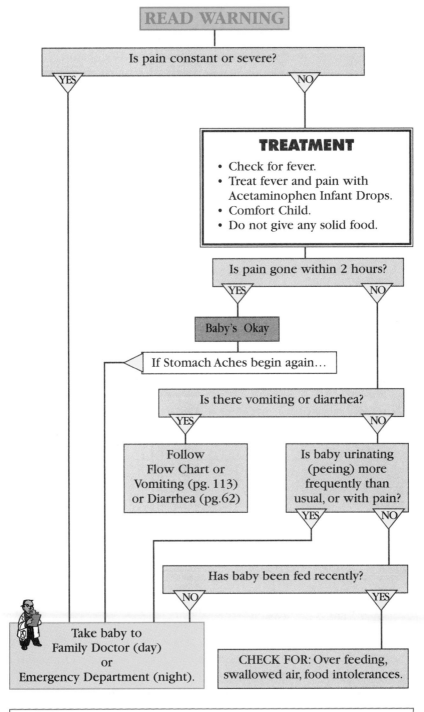

READ WARNING

Is pain constant or severe?

YES   NO

TREATMENT
- Check for fever.
- Treat fever and pain with Acetaminophen Infant Drops.
- Comfort Child.
- Do not give any solid food.

Is pain gone within 2 hours?

YES   NO

Baby's Okay

If Stomach Aches begin again…

Is there vomiting or diarrhea?

YES   NO

Follow Flow Chart or Vomiting (pg. 113) or Diarrhea (pg.62)

Is baby urinating (peeing) more frequently than usual, or with pain?

YES   NO

Has baby been fed recently?

NO   YES

Take baby to Family Doctor (day) or Emergency Department (night).

CHECK FOR: Over feeding, swallowed air, food intolerances.

Cramps are intermittent stomach pains, often relieved by vomiting or diarrhea, or with a meal between painful episodes.

STOMACH ACHES

STOMACH ACHES

Trade Secrets

- Pains that resolve within two hours are usually safe.
- Continuous pains that last beyond two hours need to be checked.
- Appendicitis pain is usually in the middle or lower right part of the abdomen. If in doubt, get it checked.
- Appendicitis is rare in children less than three years of age.
- Make sure there are no toxic plants in the house.
- Keep the "throw up bucket" nearby in case of vomiting.

Definitions

- **Constant Pain** is continuous pain; it does not come and go.
- **Cramps** are intermittent stomach pains, often relieved by vomiting or diarrhea, or with a snack or drink between painful episodes.
- **Food Intolerances** are an individual's sensitivity to certain foods leading to stomach upset.
- **Overfeeding** is stomach pain due to excessive food consumption.
- **Projectile Vomiting** is vomiting so forceful that matter is propelled several feet.
- **Stomach Aches** are defined as any discomfort felt in the abdomen.
- **Swallowed Air** is abdominal pain due to increased air intake while feeding or inefficient burping after feeding.

Synonyms

- Abdominal pain
- Belly ache
- Tummy ache

Medications/Treatments

- **Acetaminophen Infant Drops** (e.g., Tempra, Tylenol) are used to both control pain and lower fever. *Do not use ASA or aspirin.*
- **Oral Replacement Solutions** (e.g., Gastrolyte, Lytren, Pedialyte, Rehydralyte) are made to replace fluid and electrolyte losses in children with vomiting and /or diarrhea.
- Treatment depends upon the cause of the stomach pain. Most children will respond well to rest, acetaminophen and a warm water bottle.

STOMACH ACHES

SUNBURNS

Jody was 11 months old when she was brought in to the office.

"We were at a family picnic yesterday and she somehow got a sunburn on her arms and scalp," explained her mother. "She spent the day on a blanket underneath a tree so I didn't think she needed any sunscreen. I tried to keep her hat on but she just kept pulling it off. The only time she was actually out in the sun was when the relatives were passing her around. I feel terrible, she was whining all night and wouldn't eat her breakfast this morning."

Examination revealed a girl with good hydration but a first-degree burn to her scalp, arms and legs.

Jody had her first sunburn.

Unless you live in a cave, ultraviolet light exposure from the sun, much like death and taxes, is unavoidable. While death and taxes are relentless, the damaging effects of the sun can be significantly lessened with a little proactive sunscreen use.

Parents should make the use of sunscreens and bike helmets a daily ritual with their child.

SUNBURNS

SUNBURNS

SYMPTOMS

- Skin is pink or red, warm, painful, and with or without blisters
- Sunburn symptoms may not start for two or more hours
after the sun damage has occurred

GOALS

Stop the burning and treat the burn.

TIPS

- Stop the burning! Get baby out of both direct and indirect sunlight.
- Either put the child in a cool bath or wrap in a cool wet towel.
Do this regularly, especially in the first few hours.
This may help reduce the depth and extent of the burn.
- Use pediatric acetaminophen or ibuprofen for pain relief.
- Try oatmeal (Aveeno Colloidal Powder) or baking soda in
the bath to reduce discomfort.
- Use an antihistamine to reduce itchiness.
Do not administer antihistamines in children less than 6 months old
without first consulting your family doctor.
- Do not apply butter, lard, margarine, vitamin E, petroleum jelly, honey,
warm water, tea bags or sunburn anaesthetic sprays to sunburned skin.
- Wash blistered areas daily with mild soap and water, pat dry and cover
with an antibiotic ointment and a dry sterile dressing.
- Children need protection from all aspects of the sun: use eyeglasses,
hats, sun blocks for noses and lips an appropriate clothing.
Parents are role models for proper skin care; be a good example.
- Use sunscreens that block both UV-A (the skin-damaging rays) and
UV-B (the skin-burning rays). Reapply sunscreens regularly
(approximately every 2 hours). Reapply sunscreens more regularly if
child is swimming or sweating. Try the new "waterproof" sunscreens.
- Sunscreens are needed during all four seasons!
- Apply the sunscreen 20 minutes before baby is to go outside. Avoid having
children outside between 10 am and 2 pm (when sun's rays are the
strongest). Replace your sunscreens yearly.

SUNBURNS

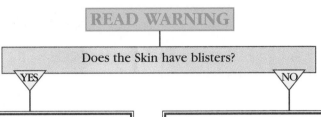

Does the Skin have blisters?

YES ▽   NO ▽

TREATMENT

- Remove baby from the sun.
- Stop the burning and cool the skin. Use cooling baths (add 1-2 tbsp. of baking soda to bath water or apply cool wet compresses to sunburned skin every 15 minutes until skin is cool.
- Increase fluid intake.
- Use pediatric acetaminophen or ibuprofen.
- Do not break the blisters.
- Apply antibiotic ointment and cover with sterile gauze dressing.
- Use an antihistamine for itch.

TREATMENT

- Remove baby from the sun.
- Stop the burning and cool the skin. Use cooling baths (add 1 to 2 tablespoons of baking soda to bath water) or apply cool wet compresses to sunburned skin every 15 minutes until skin is cool.
- Increase fluid intake.
- Use pediatric ibuprofen or acetaminophen.
- Use antihistamine for itch.
- Apply moisturizing lotion or 0.5% hydrocortisone cream to unblistered, sunburned skin.
- Apply moisturizing lotion or 0.5% hydrocortisone cream to unblistered, sunburned skin.

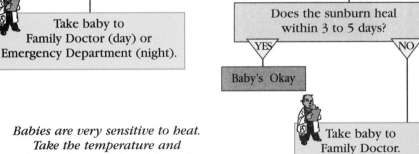

Take baby to Family Doctor (day) or Emergency Department (night).

Does the sunburn heal within 3 to 5 days?

YES ▽   NO ▽

Baby's Okay

Take baby to Family Doctor.

Babies are very sensitive to heat. Take the temperature and closely watch any baby with sunburn for symptoms of excessive heat exposure.

SIGNS OF DEHYDRATION:
• Dry mouth and tongue • Cracked lips • No tears • Sunken eyes
• No urine in six hours (or fewer than six diapers per day)
• Depressed soft spot on scalp • Lethargic
(See pg. 63 for more on dehydration)

SUNBURNS

SUNBURNS

Trade Secrets

- The best treatment for sunburn is prevention, especially in babies.
- Infants, with their thin skin, are at increased risk for burns.
- First- and second-degree burns rarely leave scars.
- To heal without scarring, prevent the burned skin from getting infected.
- Pain usually lasts for the first 48 hours. Skin peeling usually occurs within seven to 10 days of the burn.
- Burning causes dehydration, so encourage your child to drink more fluids.
- The risk of malignant melanoma doubles with each blistering sunburn.
- Infants, with their reduced ability to sweat and control their body temperature, are at increased risk for heat exhaustion and heat stroke.
- The skin is red in first-degree burns
- The skin has blisters in second-degree burns

Definitions

- **SPF** (Sun Protection Factor) is a rating scale for the protection ability of sunscreens. SPF-15 gives you 15 times as much protection as your natural skin coloring.
- **Sunburn** is the burning of the skin, lips, etc., as a result of excessive sun (ultraviolet light) exposure.

Synonyms

- Burned
- Burnt
- Cooked
- Fried
- Lobsterized
- Scorched
- Toasted

Medications/Treatments

- **Lip Balms** with UV protection.
- **Sunscreens** with UV-A and UV-B blocking (e.g., Ombrelle, Photoplex, PreSun). Purchase sunscreens with an SPF designation of 15 or higher.
- **Zinc Creams** are excellent for protecting noses, lips and tips of ears.
- **Ibuprofen** (e.g., Infant Advil, Infant Motrin) may both treat the pain and reduce the depth or extent of the burn by reducing skin inflammation.
- **Antihistamines** (e.g., Benadryl, Claritin) are used to reduce the discomfort of itch. Do not administer antihistamines in children less than 6 months old without first consulting your family doctor.

SUNBURNS

TEETHING PROBLEMS

Ali was six months old when she was brought in to the office.

"She just hasn't been herself for the past few days," her mother explained. "She has been irritable and drooling excessively. She has been running a low-grade fever and is chewing on everything that she can get her little hands on. She has been extremely clingy and wants to be held all the time. She was up half the night and today she started to rub her ears. I thought I had better bring her in to check for an ear infection."

On examination, Ali appeared healthy without any indication of infection, including ear infection. She had a rash on her chin and a small white spot was evident on her lower gums where her central incisor was coming through.

Ali was having teething problems.

Breast-feeding mothers often have the inside track on knowing when their babies are developing teeth.

TEETHING PROBLEMS

TEETHING PROBLEMS

SYMPTOMS

• Chewing on everything • Fever below 38.5°C (101.3°F)
• Flushed cheeks • Drooling • Finger sucking • Restlessness
• Jaw grinding • Mild irritability • Decreased appetite

GOALS

Reduce pain and make teething period easier for child and parent.

TIPS

- Most children begin to develop teeth at about six months
  (see First Teeth Chart, page 107).
- Teething discomfort differs between children.
  Many babies have no pain at all with teething.
- Some symptoms may appear one or two months before teeth erupt.
- Try soft frozen foods for infant to chew on
  (frozen waffle or bagel, popsicle) or a frozen teething ring.
- Try freezing a wet wash cloth for your baby to chew on.
- Massage or rub gums with a freshly washed finger or piece of ice for
  a minute or so.
- Cleaning teeth and gums is important for babies too! Use a gauze pad
  or very soft child's toothbrush to clean after bottle or breast feeding.
- Start early to make gum and tooth cleaning a regular part of baby's
  daily routine. The sooner you start the less of a battle you will get.
- DO NOT USE: alcohol, coins or thimbles on your baby's gums to assist
  with teething.
- Look in the baby's mouth. You should see a slight swelling or whitish
  area where the tooth is coming through. You can also feel the tooth
  before it erupts.

TEETHING PROBLEMS

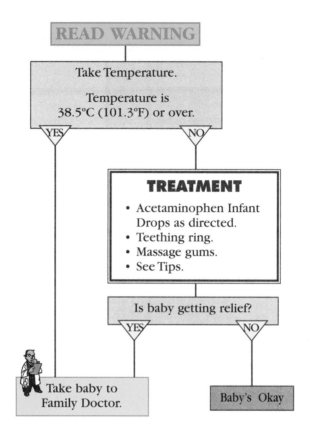

READ WARNING

Take Temperature.

Temperature is
38.5°C (101.3°F) or over.

YES NO

TREATMENT

- Acetaminophen Infant
  Drops as directed.
- Teething ring.
- Massage gums.
- See Tips.

Is baby getting relief?

YES NO

Take baby to
Family Doctor.

Baby's Okay

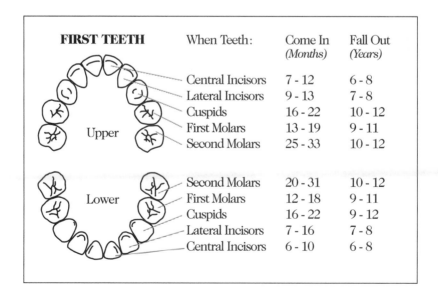

FIRST TEETH	When Teeth:	Come In (Months)	Fall Out (Years)
Central Incisors		7 - 12	6 - 8
Lateral Incisors		9 - 13	7 - 8
Cuspids		16 - 22	10 - 12
First Molars		13 - 19	9 - 11
Upper — Second Molars		25 - 33	10 - 12
Second Molars		20 - 31	10 - 12
First Molars		12 - 18	9 - 11
Lower — Cuspids		16 - 22	9 - 12
Lateral Incisors		7 - 16	7 - 8
Central Incisors		6 - 10	6 - 8

TEETHING PROBLEMS

Trade Secrets

- Teething is often wrongly blamed for everything from fevers to diaper rash.
- Most children have no pain or other complicating symptoms when developing new teeth.
- Normal children may have delayed development of teeth until after 12 months of age, but the average is 5 to 7 months for the first tooth eruption.
- Baby girls often develop teeth before baby boys.
- Development of teeth often occurs at the same time between siblings.
- There is usually no problem when teething is later than normal.
- Babies born with a tooth need to see a dentist as soon as possible.
- Babies born prematurely will often show a slight delay in teething.

Definitions

- **Deciduous Teeth** (or primary teeth) are the 20 teeth that babies develop. They are later replaced by 32 adult teeth.
- **Erupts** – when a tooth pokes through the gum.
- **Low-Grade Temperature** is one below 38.5°C (101.3°F).
- **Teething** refers to the eruption of deciduous teeth in children.

Synonyms

- None

Medications/Treatments

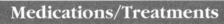

- **Acetaminophen Infant Drops** (e.g., Tempra, Tylenol) are used to both control pain and lower fever.
  Do not use ASA or aspirin.
- **Analgesic Teething Gels / Solutions** (e.g., Orajel, Anbesol) are over-the-counter treatments for relief of the pain of teething. Check with your family doctor before using these products.
- **Anti-inflammatories** (e.g., Pediatric, Advil or Motrin) are used to control pain, inflammation and lower fever.

THRUSH

CASE STUDY

Jordan was brought in to the office for his regular well-baby examination at two months of age.

During the visit his mother mentioned he had not been eating as well as usual. "The past few days he seems to have lost interest in breast feeding," his mother said. "He doesn't seem to feed as long as usual. Do you think he is getting enough milk or is he just trying to wean himself?"

The examination showed he was his normal, healthy, robust self and his growth and development were right on track. However, a quick look in the mouth showed white patches stuck to the gums, tongue and cheeks.

"It looks like Jordan may have developed a case of thrush," I told mom. "I thought those were just milk curds," she exclaimed.

I showed her how the patches couldn't be removed with a piece of gauze. Unlike milk, these white patches stick to the inside of the mouth.

Jordan had his first case of thrush.

When a child with a previously healthy appetite suddenly stops eating, the cause is often found by shedding some light in the child's mouth.

THRUSH

THRUSH

SYMPTOMS

- Irritable • Decreased appetite or reluctance to feed
- White patches in mouth and on tongue in either a bottle-fed or breast-fed baby

GOALS

Determine if problem is thrush and treat baby.

TIPS

- If baby has thrush, breast-feeding mothers should clean their nipples with mild soap and water and apply antifungal cream after each feeding (see your pharmacist or doctor). Wash nipples with soap and water before feeding to remove the cream.
- Reduce feeding time to 20 to 30 minutes maximum per feeding. This may increase the frequency of feedings but reduce baby's, and your, discomfort.
- If sucking seems painful, try using a cup and /or spoon.
- Use baby foods that are soft and easily chewed and swallowed.
- Sterilize baby bottle nipples and soothers by boiling in water for 10 minutes. Be sure to allow them to cool before giving to baby.
- Eliminate soother (pacifier) if possible.
- Babies with thrush are at higher risk for diaper rash (see Diaper Rash, page 57). Watch for it.
- See your family doctor for treatment of thrush symptoms in mouth, or for recurrent thrush infections.

THRUSH

THRUSH

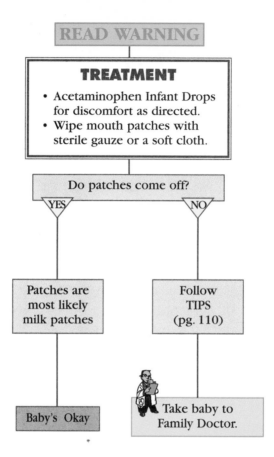

TREATMENT

- Acetaminophen Infant Drops for discomfort as directed.
- Wipe mouth patches with sterile gauze or a soft cloth.

Do patches come off?

YES   NO

Patches are most likely milk patches

Follow TIPS (pg. 110)

Baby's Okay

Take baby to Family Doctor.

THRUSH

Trade Secrets

- Thrush is a common problem in both breast-fed and bottle-fed babies. It is caused by the yeast called Candida and is easily treated with medicine by your family doctor.
- Thrush may or may not cause painful sucking for the baby.
- Thrush may or may not cause painful nipples in breastfeeding moms.
- Thrush is often present with a yeast type diaper rash. Watch for it.
- Babies with thrush do not need to stop breast feeding.
- Babies with thrush do not need to switch to cow's milk.
- Sterilize the bottle nipples and tips of soothers both at the beginning and at the end of treatment to prevent recurrent bouts of thrush.

Definitions

- **Candida** is a yeast (fungus) that is the most common cause of thrush.
- **Recurrent Thrush Infections** are those that keep recurring despite treatment.
- **Resistant Thrush** infections are those that do not get better with normal treatments.
- **Thrush** is a fungal infection in the mouth.
- **Weaning** is the conversion of baby from breastfeeding to other nutrition (including solids and/or bottle feeding).

Synonyms

- Monilia
- Mucocutaneous candidiasis
- Oropharyngeal candidiasis

Medications/Treatments

- **Acetaminophen Infant Drops** (e.g., Tempra, Tylenol) are used to both control both pain and lower fever. *Do not use ASA or aspirin.*
- **Antifungal Creams** are often used on the mother's nipples to treat for fungal infection and prevent recurrent thrush in babies.
- **Gentian Violet** is a purple colored medicine that is painted on the inside of baby's mouth when normal treatments do not work.
- **Nystatin Antifungal Oral Suspension** is frequently prescribed by your doctor for treatment of this condition. This is used in baby's mouth.

THRUSH

VOMITING

Bart was nine months old when he was brought to the emergency department.

"He hasn't been able to keep anything down in the past two days," his exasperated mother said. "I'm worried that he may be dehydrated. Everything I try to feed him he just throws up. He won't even take his formula and he usually loves his formula. He is also much more clingy, is sleeping more than usual and has been running a temperature for the last two days. He just doesn't seem right."

Examination revealed a quiet and dehydrated infant (his mouth and tongue were dry and he hadn't produced a wet diaper for more than six hours). He had a temperature over 38.5°C (101.3°F) and looked and acted sick.

For Bart, this was his first illness causing vomiting.

Bart required admission to hospital for intravenous fluids.

Almost anything can induce vomiting in children, even an illness.

A 'throw-up bucket' is a friend every family with children will need

VOMITING

SYMPTOMS

- "Sick to the stomach" with repeated retching or throwing up

GOALS

Comfort child and prevent dehydration.

TIPS

- For the first six hours, offer a tablespoon of oral replacement solution every 15 minutes. If baby vomits, wait one hour then start again. If no vomiting after the first hour try 2 tablespoons every 15 minutes.
- Oral replacement solutions are made especially for children with vomiting or diarrhea. Do not use sugary drinks such as soda pop, fruit drinks, juice, sweet tea, etc.
- For vomiting that continues beyond six hours take your child to your family doctor or the Emergency Department.
- For vomiting that stops at or before six hours try the following: (These will depend upon the age of your baby).
  - When vomiting stops try to restart regular formula or whole milk.
  - Do not give solid foods until vomiting stops.
  - When vomiting stops, try a graduated age-appropriate diet. Example: the **BRAT** diet (**B**ananas, **R**ice, **A**pple sauce, **T**oast). Cereal, crackers and pablum are also okay if age-appropriate.
- Most children resume their regular diet within 12 to 24 hours.
- Vomiting most commonly occurs with an intestinal infection (gastroenteritis). It is also common with ear, throat or urinary tract infections, bowel obstructions and hernias.
- Spitting up is the effortless bringing up of two or three mouthfuls. Vomiting is the forceful evacuation of most of the stomach contents.
- If baby has repeated or projectile vomiting, see your family doctor.

VOMITING

VOMITING

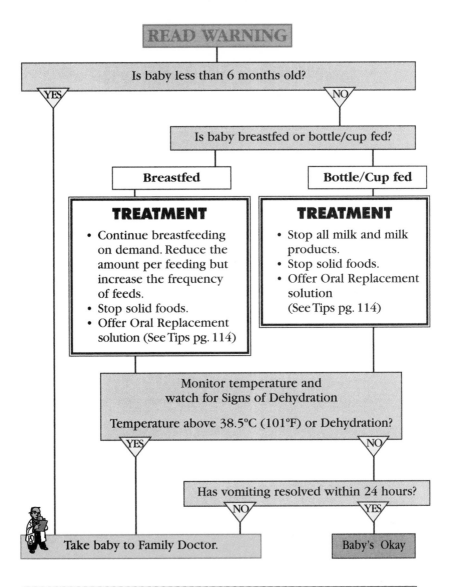

Is baby less than 6 months old?

YES | NO

Is baby breastfed or bottle/cup fed?

Breastfed

Bottle/Cup fed

TREATMENT

- Continue breastfeeding on demand. Reduce the amount per feeding but increase the frequency of feeds.
- Stop solid foods.
- Offer Oral Replacement solution (See Tips pg. 114)

TREATMENT

- Stop all milk and milk products.
- Stop solid foods.
- Offer Oral Replacement solution (See Tips pg. 114)

Monitor temperature and watch for Signs of Dehydration

Temperature above 38.5°C (101°F) or Dehydration?

YES | NO

Has vomiting resolved within 24 hours?

NO | YES

Take baby to Family Doctor.

Baby's Okay

SIGNS OF DEHYDRATION
- Dry mouth and tongue • Cracked lips • No tears • Sunken eyes
- No urine in 6 hours (or less than 6 diapers per day)
- Depressed soft spot on scalp • Lethargic

FLUIDS TO USE IN INFANTS
Oral Replacement Solutions are made especially for children with vomiting or diarrhea

FLUIDS TO AVOID IN INFANTS
Sugary drinks such as:
soda pop, fruit drinks, juice, sweat tea, etc.

VOMITING

VOMITING

Trade Secrets

- Drink, drink, drink. Vomiting in children can quickly lead to dehydration, especially if associated with diarrhea or any other symptoms of illness.
- The younger the child the closer you should watch for signs of dehydration.
- Use your parental intuition. If your child looks or acts sick, or if you feel something is wrong, get them checked by a doctor.
- Most physicians will recommend seeing an infant with vomiting every 24 to 48 hours to check for possible dehydration and weight loss.
- Vomiting after a head injury may be a sign of a brain injury and needs an assessment by a doctor.
- Almost any illness can cause vomiting in children. It may be the only presenting symptom.
- Infants that are lethargic are often at least 5 – 10% dehydrated.

Definitions

- **Breastfeeding on Demand** is breastfeeding whenever the baby seems hungry.
- **Coffee Ground Emesis** is vomit that contains blood.
- **Dehydration** is an excessive loss of body water.
- **Lethargic** is a child that is more sleepy/drowsy than usual.
- **Vomiting, or Emesis**, is the forcible expulsion of stomach contents through the mouth.

Synonyms

- Barf
- Emesis
- Puke
- Regurgitate
- Retch
- Throw up
- Up-chuck

Medications/Treatments

- **Acetaminophen** (e.g. Tylenol, Tempra) is used foe fever or pain. This can be administered by mouth or suppository.
- **Antiemetics** (e.g., Gravol) are sometimes used to treat nausea and vomiting in children. They are given by mouth, injection or suppository. Consult with your doctor first before using for correct dosage.
- **Diagnostic Tests** (blood work, urine tests, X Rays, ultrasounds)are often needed to evaluate the cause or effect of vomiting.
- **Oral Replacement Solutions** (e.g., Gastrolyte, Lytren, Pedialyte) are especially made to replace the fluid and electrolyte losses in children with vomiting and/or diarrhea.

VOMITING

Caring for a Sick Child

Tips for Treating Sick Babies

THE 3As RULE

A sick baby shows one or more of three main changes:

- Change in **A**ppetite (usually decreases).
- Change in **A**ctivity (usually diminishes).
- Change in **A**ttitude (previously happy baby may become irritable or withdrawn).

Infants can't communicate verbally, so we must watch for these changes. Parents are best able to tell when their child is sick. This book will help you identify and, in most cases, treat common infant illnesses.

HOW TO TAKE THE "YUCK" OUT OF MEDICINE

- Blow on the face of a child under one year. The baby will respond by holding his or her breath for a second, then swallow.
- Chill liquid medicine to reduce the taste sensation.
- Provide a treat or tasty drink after the medicine to mask any aftertaste. Mix the medicine with a spoonful of juice, pudding or apple sauce to hide the taste.
  (DO NOT put medicine in a whole bottle of juice or formula.)
- NEVER microwave medicine!
- Ask your doctor about the taste of the medicine prescribed. Ask that they prescribe the better-tasting medicine, if possible.

FEEDING A SICK CHILD

Unless your doctor has recommended a special diet, or in cases of vomiting or diarrhea, let your child eat and drink what he or she wants when ill (as long as they are healthy, nutritious choices).

- You may want to give smaller and more frequent feedings to a sick baby.
- Encourage a sick baby to drink fluids whenever possible.

Home First-Aid Kit

Every home should have a first-aid kit containing items appropriate for the ages of the family members. The contents will change somewhat as a result of changes in age. The first-aid kit should be stored out of the reach of children, yet in a location that it is readily accessible when you need it. Often a good place is the closet shelf by the back door. The first-aid kit contents should be focused on injuries. The first-med kit (which we will discuss on the next page) should be focused on illness.

A first-aid kit in a baby's home should contain at least the following:

- **Adhesive Tape** For dressing wounds (use with gauze)

- **Antibiotic cream** Cream for burns, cuts and scrapes

- **Bandage closures** In 5 millimeter (1/4 inch) and 2.5 centimeter (1 inch) sizes for taping edges of cuts together. (Also called "butterfly closures")

- **Bandages** Assorted sizes for minor cuts & scrapes

- **Child-safe ice bags** For injuries and treating fever

- **First-Aid Manual** For basic first aid advice and guidance

- **Gauze** In 5 and 10 centimeter (2 and 4 inch) widths for dressing wounds

- **Gel pack** Can be used as a cold or warm pack

- **Gloves** Vinyl or latex for protecting hands and reducing the risk of infection when treating open wounds

- **Safety pins** For fastening splints, slings & bandages

- **Scissors** With rounded tips

- **Telfa pads** Non-stick dressing for wounds

- **Triangular bandage** For wrapping bandages and making an arm sling

- **Tweezers & needle** For removing small splinters and ticks

Home First-Med Kit

Every home should have a first-med kit containing medications and supplies that are needed for treating common medical conditions. This kit will obviously change depending on the ages of the family members. This kit should be locked and stored in a location that is not accessible to children, as should all medications. Keep a copy of Your Home Doctor™ Babies in a handy location or with the kit so that you have access to it when you need it (usually at 3 in the morning). By combining the book with the following list of over-the-counter medications you have the tools necessary (both the information and treatment tools) to treat your child to the best of your ability.

The first-med kit for baby should contain the following:

• **Acetaminophen infant drops**	For fever and pain
• **Antibiotic cream or ointment**	For burns, scrapes, cuts & skin infections
• **Antihistamines**	For allergic reactions and itch
• **Decongestant infant drops**	For allergies and colds
• **Gripe water**	For colic and stomach cramps
• **Nasal aspirator**	For suctioning plugged noses
• **Oral replacement solution or powder**	For diarrhea, vomiting and dehydration
• **Penlight**	For illumination
• **Saline nose drops**	For nasal congestion & colds
• **Simethicone drops**	For colic and stomach cramps
• **Sunscreen**	To prevent sunburn
• **Thermometer**	For checking the temperature
• **Zinc oxide barrier cream**	For diaper rash

Home First-Med Kit

Infant/Child CPR

The Heart and Stroke Foundation of Canada sets the guidelines for cardio-pulmonary resuscitation (CPR) and emergency cardiac care in Canada. Their techniques for CPR are summarized on the following pages.

CPR is an emergency procedure used when a person is not breathing and their heart stops beating. CPR alone does not save lives; the purpose of CPR is to keep the victim's brain and heart supplied with blood and oxygen until medical help arrives.

The Heart and Stroke Foundation of Canada offers an Infant / Child course in CPR that trains people to recognize and react to emergency situations. The course also teaches parents and childcare workers how to prevent childhood injuries, assess risk factors, and how to keep blood and oxygen flowing when the heart stops beating or there is an airway obstruction. While CPR can be used on people of all ages, the material in this book focuses on specific techniques for infants and children. For CPR, a child is considered to be anyone between the ages of one and eight and an infant is a child less than one-year old.

After completing an Infant / Child course, parents and childcare workers will be able to provide CPR until Emergency Medical Services (EMS) arrive. The EMS system is a community-wide system for responding to sudden illness or injury. It may include ambulance services, paramedics, police, fire fighters and other people trained in first-aid and emergency action. Find out the telephone number for the Poison Control Centre and the EMS system in your community and keep it close to each telephone. In many places the EMS number is 911; in other areas, a seven-digit telephone number is used.

With training in CPR, you become an important part of the EMS system. Review these techniques regularly, and update your skills by taking a CPR course each year.

Reproduced with permission
Copyright Infant / Child Performance Guidelines for CPR, 1994,
Heart and Stroke Foundation of Canada

Infant CPR
One-Rescuer

1 Determine unresponsiveness.

If another person is available,
have them call the EMS system.

2 Open airway using head tilt/chin lift.

Check breathing for 3 to 5 seconds.
1. **Look** at the chest and stomach for rise
   and fall movement.
2. **Listen** for sounds of breathing.
3. **Feel** for exhaled breath on your cheek.
   If the infant is breathing on their own,
   place in recovery position on their side.

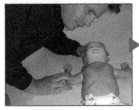

**3 Give 2 slow breaths
(1 to 1.5 seconds per breath).**

Watch chest rise.
Allow for exhalation between breaths.

4 Check brachial pulse for 5 to 10 secs.

If breathing is absent but pulse is present,
provide rescue breathing (1 breath every
3 seconds, about 20 breaths per minute).

**5 If no pulse, give 5 chest compressions
followed by 1 slow breath; 5:1 cycle.**

Rate of at least 100 compressions per min;
compress at a depth of 1 to 2.5
centimeters (1/2 to 1 inch).

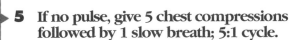

**6 If rescuer is alone, call the EMS system
after about 1 minute of CPR.**

**7 Check pulse and breathing for
3 to 5 seconds.**

If no pulse and no breathing, continue 5:1
cycle beginning with chest compressions.
Check for return of pulse and spontaneous
breathing every few minutes.

Infant CPR

Infant Foreign-Body Airway Obstruction

If the child is conscious, or changes from conscious to unconscious

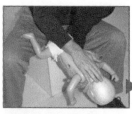

1 Observe the infant for:
- weak cry
- high-pitched noise
- difficulty breathing

2 Give up to 5 back blows and up to 5 chest thrusts.

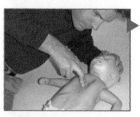

3 Repeat back blows and chest thrusts until effective or until infant becomes unconscious.

4 If another person is available have him or her call the EMS system.

5 Perform tongue-jaw lift only if you see the object.

Perform finger sweep to try to remove the object.

6 Open the airway and try to ventilate.

If still obstructed, reposition head and try to ventilate again.

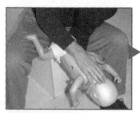

7 If still obstructed, give up to 5 back blows and up to 5 chest thrusts.

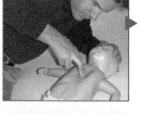

8 Repeat sequence 5 through 7, until effective or medical help arrives.

If the infant is breathing or starts breathing, place in recovery position on their side.

9 If alone and airway obstruction is not relieved, call the EMS system after about 1 minute.

122

Infant Foreign-Body Airway Obstruction

If the child is found unconscious

1 **Determine unresponsiveness.**

If another person is available, have them call the EMS system.

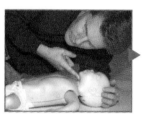

2 **Open airway using head tilt/chin lift. Check breathing for 3 to 5 seconds.**

1. **Look** at the chest and stomach for rise and fall movement.
2. **Listen** for sounds of breathing.
3. **Feel** for exhaled breath on your cheek.

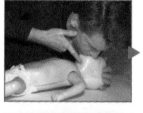

3 **Give 2 slow breaths (1 to 1.5 seconds per breath).**

If air does not go in on the first breath, reposition head and try to ventilate again.

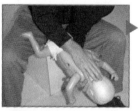

4 **If obstructed, give up to 5 back blows and up to 5 chest thrusts.**

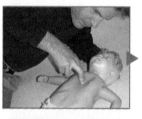

5 **Perform tongue-jaw lift only if you see the object.**

Perform finger sweep to try to remove the object.

6 **Repeat sequence 3 through 5, until effective or medical help arrives.**

If the infant is breathing, or starts breathing on their own, place in recovery position on his or her side.

7 **If alone and airway obstruction is not relieved, call EMS system after about 1 minute.**

Airway Obstruction/Infant

Child CPR / One-Rescuer

Check the scene. Coming upon a collapsed child can be a frightening experience. You want to ensure that the rescue attempt is as safe and effective as possible. You should take charge, assess hazards for yourself and others, and make sure that the area is safe. Initial caution may prevent other injuries. Hazards may include electrical wires, fire or gas leakages.

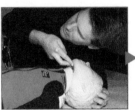

1 Determine unresponsiveness.

If another person is available, have them call the EMS system.

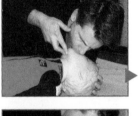

2 Open airway, using head tilt/chin lift. Check breathing for 3 to 5 seconds.

1. **Look** at the chest and stomach for movement (rise and fall).
2. **Listen** for sounds of breathing.
3. **Feel** for exhaled breath on your cheek. If the child is breathing or starts breathing on his/her own, place in recovery position on his/her side.

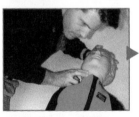

3 Give 2 slow breaths (1 to 1.5 seconds per breath).

Watch chest rise. Allow for exhalation between breaths.

4 Check carotid pulse for 5 to 10 secs.

If breathing is absent but pulse is present, provide rescue breathing (1 breath every 3 seconds, about 20 breaths per minute).

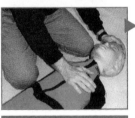

5 If no pulse, give 5 chest compressions, followed by 1 slow breath; 5:1 cycle.

Compress at a rate of 100 compressions per min; compress at a depth of 2.5 to 4 centimeters (1 to 1.5 inches).

6 If rescuer is alone, call the EMS system after about 1 minute of CPR.

7 Check pulse & breathing for 3 to 5 secs.

If no pulse and no breathing, continue 5:1 cycle beginning with chest compressions. Check for return of pulse and spontaneous breathing every few minutes.

Child CPR

Child Foreign-Body Airway Obstruction

*If the child is conscious, or changes from
conscious to unconscious*

1 Ask, "Are you choking?"

> If the child can speak, breathe or
> cough, do not interfere.

2 Give abdominal thrusts if the
child cannot speak, breathe or
cough.

3 Repeat thrusts until effective,
or until the child becomes
unconscious.

4 If another person is available,
have him or her call the EMS
system.

5 Perform tongue-jaw lift only
if you see the object.

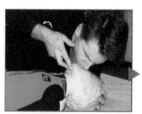

> Perform finger sweep to try to
> remove the object.

6 Open the airway and try to
ventilate.

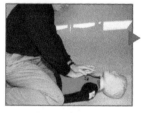

> If still obstructed, reposition head
> and try to ventilate again.

7 If still obstructed, give up to
5 abdominal thrusts.

8 Repeat sequence 5 through 7,
until effective or medical help
arrives.

> If the child is breathing or starts
> breathing on their own, place in
> recovery position on their side.

9 If alone and airway obstruction is
not relieved, call the EMS system
after about 1 minute.

Child Foreign-Body Airway Obstruction

If the child is found unconscious

1 **Determine unresponsiveness.**

If another person is available,
have them call the EMS system.

2 **Open airway, using head tilt/chin lift.
Check breathing for 3 to 5 seconds.**

1. **Look** at the chest and stomach for
   rise and fall movement.
2. **Listen** for sounds of breathing.
3. **Feel** for exhaled breath on your
   cheek.

3 **Give 2 slow breaths (1 to 1.5 seconds
per breath).**

If air does not go in on the first breath,
reposition head and try to ventilate again.

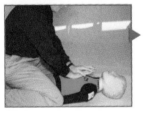

4 **If obstructed, give up to 5 abdominal
thrusts.**

5 **Perform tongue-jaw lift only if you
see the object.**

Perform finger sweep to try to remove
the object.

6 **Repeat sequence 3 through 5, until
effective or medical help arrives.**

If the child is breathing or starts
breathing on their own, place in
recovery position on their side.

(911

7 **If alone and airway obstruction is
not relieved, call the EMS system
after about 1 minute.**

Childproofing

An Ounce of Prevention

"An ounce of prevention is worth a pound of cure."

Nowhere is this more true than in danger prevention in the newborn to two-year-old age group.

The list of potential dangers to children in this age group is unending. The world is their oyster and they usually try to open every shell. Therefore, the list of dos and don'ts are also endless. In the following pages are some of the most common areas of concern. Included as well are some areas not thought of as dangerous, and to adults they are not, but to the under-two-year-old, they provide an extra avenue of danger.

The greatest dangers to your child in the newborn to 2 yr age range are:

- **Choking**
- **Falls**
- **Burns**
- **Drowning**
- **Poisoning**
- **Suffocation / Strangulation**

Every room has its own potential dangers for a child. Each development stage provides changing physical and intellectual resources to explore these dangers. Coupled with a child's natural curiosity about their environment, this provides enough potential danger to give a parent an anxiety attack. Rather than fostering further paranoia, a state commonly shared by all parents of small children, take time to see the world from a child's perspective.

Every three months or so, explore your child's environment from his or her point of view. This means getting down on your hands and knees and crawling around their space. This may seem odd and your spouse may laugh at you, but they will respect your conscientiousness when you arise with that piece of Lego, coin, peanut or piece of popcorn. Even the smallest things can be of danger to young children. Find them before they do. Generally speaking, if something is less than 2.5 centimeters (1 inch) it is small enough to put in a mouth and choke upon.

Most important, sharpen your parental intuition skills. This includes becoming expert in danger detection for your child as well as becoming a medically prepared parent. You must learn to be prepared for both accidents and illness. All parents should learn basic first aid, CPR and stop-choking techniques. Call the Heart and Stroke Foundation or St. John Ambulance to find the infant CPR course location nearest you.

Be aware and be prepared!

Childproofing
In General

- Learn infant CPR and infant/child stop-choking techniques.
- Learn basic first aid techniques.
- Put all medicines and vitamins in a secure, locked cupboard.
- Secure all detergents, cleaning products, bleach and breakables in high or locked cupboards.
- Always use a sunblock (SPF-15 or greater).
- Use the security straps on all change tables, strollers and highchairs.
- Place the baby in a playpen when you are busy (in the bathroom, making supper, talking on the phone, etc.).
- Dress your child in fireproof clothing.
- Avoid foods at high risk for choking (hot dogs, raw vegetables, hard candies, nuts and popcorn).
- Never leave an infant unsupervised with an animal, regardless of how much you trust the animal or the infant.
- Teach your child early how best to treat animals.
- Do not allow animals to sleep in your child's room.
- Never leave an infant unattended, especially if around water (bucket, toilet, pool, tub, stream, ditch, puddle, well, cistern, pond, lake, ocean, etc.).
- Avoid the use of all baby walkers.
- Never allow children to play with balloons without supervision.
- Do not smoke around children or in a child's house.
- Tie all plastic grocery bags and dry cleaning bags in a knot before discarding.
- Keep all drapery cords out of reach.
- Block off all staircases and stairwells.
- Have your house plants checked. Make sure that they are non-toxic.
- Keep matches, lighters and fuel out of reach.
- Beware of stoves, ovens, barbeques, as well as fire (both in fireplaces or open air).
- Never assume your child is "old enough to know better."

Childproofing
The Car

- Always check behind and under your vehicle before you back up, no matter how busy you are.
- Always remove your keys from the ignition.
- Never leave a child unattended in a vehicle (whether running or not).
- Do not allow a vehicle to be used as a play toy.
- Do not let children play around vehicles.
- Use a towel to cover the buckles and seats on hot days to prevent burns.
- Purchase all new vehicles with child safety devices. Use them.
- Always use the appropriate sized car seat.
- Always use the car seat tether strap to better secure the car seat to the vehicle.
- Avoid seating children in the front seat of a vehicle that has a passenger-side air bag. (Ask your car dealer).
- Many new pick-up trucks have a switch to turn off the passenger-side air bag.
- Never secure both an adult and child with the same seat belt.
- Use door and window locks if available.
- The safest position in a vehicle is the closest to the middle of the vehicle.
- Beware of children eating hard candies, suckers, popcorn of any other choking hazard while in a moving vehicle.
- Above all, use seat belts for everyone in the vehicle.

Childproofing
The House

- Danger-proof your home before the baby comes home.
- Learn to anticipate each new development stage and danger-proof in anticipation.
- Poison-proof your home: remove all detergents, cleaners, bleach, medicines, alcohol, vitamins, moth balls, paints, etc. Put them out of the reach of children and lock them away.
- Pills, medicines and vitamins often look like candy. Keep them out of reach.
- Keep your local poison control centre number on or near the phone.
- Use infant gates, cupboard locks, door handle locks, drawer locks, electric outlet protectors, corner protectors, fireplace guards, stove guards and toilet protectors.
- Place a smoke detector and fire extinguisher on every level of the house. Detectors should be placed outside all bedrooms. Check the batteries monthly and change the batteries (at least) yearly.
- A carbon monoxide detector may also be of value.
- Never leave a child unattended on a balcony.
- Secure all second-floor (and higher) windows.
- Check whether house plants are toxic.
- Anchor all bookcases to prevent them from being pulled over.
- Use sliding glass door decals and screen door snap-ons.
- Tie all cords from window blinds and curtains so that they are out of reach of children. Or cut them or cleat them.
- Use seat straps in all shopping carts, highchairs, booster seats, strollers, etc.
- Lock away all firearms and ammunition. Keep firearms separate from ammunition.
- Keep all plastic bags out of the reach of children.
- Put away all small figurines and ornaments that may pose a choking hazard during your child's early years.
- Keep alcohol out of reach and /or locked away.
- Remove the doors to all unused freezers and refrigerators.
- Buy or make a first-aid kit and first-medical kit for your home, cottage, car, etc. Keep the first-med kit locked away with all the other medications.

Childproofing
The Kitchen

- Kitchens are one of the most dangerous rooms in the house for a child.
- Secure all reachable drawers and cupboards using childproof locks.
- Protect your child from all dangling cords and hot liquids.
- Many new appliances now have child-safe electric cords.
- Turn all handles of pots and pans towards the rear of the stove. Cook on the back burners if possible.
- Use stove protectors, including stove knob covers and stove shields. Alternatively, remove all stove knobs.
- Be especially careful when using open flame cooking when children are around.
- Always keep a fire extinguisher present.
- Keep all sharp articles (knives, scissors, etc.) out of reach.
- Do not use place mats or table cloths when children are young.
- Avoid using the microwave to heat baby food or formula.
- Poison-proof under the sink. Lock away all detergents, dishwasher powder and oven cleaners.
- Keep the appliances closed when not in use.
- Use a safety latch on the refrigerator, freezer, dishwasher, microwave, trash compactor and oven.
- Store all breakables out of the reach of children, both in and out of the fridge.
- Beware of fridge magnets. They are very attractive to children and are often choking hazards.
- Store all plastic bags out of the reach of children.
- Keep your trash container in a cupboard that locks. Alternatively, have a cover that locks or seals tightly.
- Place pet food and water out of the reach of children.
- Keep the numbers of your doctor, poison control centre, hospital, dentist, police and fire department on or near the telephone.
- Keep plug protectors on all unused electric outlets.
- Allow your child a cupboard of their own with safe plastic bowls, spoons, etc.
- Use a playpen in the kitchen for your baby when cooking or on the phone.

Childproofing
The Bathroom

- Never leave a child unattended in a bathroom for any reason at any time.
- Make sure that the bathroom door can be unlocked from the outside.
- Poison-proof the medicine cabinet to make it a non-medicine cabinet.
- Put a safety lock on the medicine cabinet.
- Lock up all cosmetics, cleaners (drain and toilet), soap (especially bars), cotton balls and swabs, toothpaste, shampoos, scissors, nail clippers, nail files, fragrances, razor blades and aerosol spray cans.
- Unplug and store all electric appliances after each use.
- Use only battery-operated radios and televisions in the bathroom.
- Install ground-fault circuit interrupters (GFCI) in bathroom outlets. These help protect against electrocution.
- Use cupboard locks, drawer locks and electric outlet protectors.
- Use non-slip mats, spout covers and scald savers or faucet protectors.
- Always check the bath temperature before placing a child in the tub.
- Set the temperature on your water heater to a maximum of 49°C (120°F).
- Put a lock on the toilet lid. Close the lid after each use.

Childproofing
The Bedroom/Nursery

- Make sure that your crib conforms to safety regulations (this means that all crib slats should be no more than 6 centimeters (2-3/8 inches) apart and the corner post no higher than 1/16 inch above the end panel, or has no posts at all).
- Keep the crib away from heat vents, radiators, air conditioners and windows.
- Lower the crib and remove the bumper pads and mobiles as soon as your baby starts to stand.
- Do not leave babies unsupervised with fluffy quilts, pillows and comforters in the crib.
- Limit the number of stuffed toys in the crib.
- Make sure the mattress fits snugly in the crib and has an approved mattress liner.
- Never place a baby on a waterbed.
- Never leave a baby unattended on a change table. Always use the restraint strap on the change table.
- Use a diaper pail that has a locking lid.
- Use a toy box without a lid.
- Keep all baby cleaning products out of the reach of children.

Childproofing
The Garage

- Never leave a child unattended in the garage.
- Never store poisons or chemicals in pop bottles or any other container that may be mistaken by a child as a food or drink container.
- Keep children away from all machinery (lawn mowers, weedwackers, etc.) whether running or not.
- Keep all pesticides, poisons, cleaners, fuels, oils, antifreeze, drain and toilet cleaners, gasoline, paint and paint thinners, fertilizers, etc., locked away at all times.
- Empty all buckets and turn them upside down.
- Keep all power tools unplugged when not in use.
  Keep all power tools out of reach of children.
- Mount the garage door opener on the wall high enough to be out of reach.
- A garage door automatic return mechanism is mandatory.
- Use garbage cans with lids.
- Secure all shelving to the wall.
- Hang all rakes, shovels, etc. out of reach.

Childproofing
The Yard

- Keep the fence and gates in good repair.
- Make sure that all gate latches are out of the reach of younger children.
- Check to make sure that none of the plants or shrubs in your yard are poisonous.
- Do not use fertilizers, pesticides or herbicides around the yard when you have young children.
- Special care must be taken to secure all wells, cisterns, rain barrels and septic tanks.
- Keep children away from all running lawn mowers, weedwackers, chain saws, etc.
- Be especially vigilant with children around streams, creeks, fountains and fish ponds.
- Cover all sand boxes to prevent them from being a toilet for neighborhood animals.
- Be especially careful with barbecues and children.
- Supervise children using play equipment.
  Do not dress them in clothing with hoods and drawstrings.

Childproofing
The Pool

- Drowning is the second most common cause of death of children in some countries. Do not leave a child unattended around a pool of any size, at any age, at any time.
- Surround the pool with an approved safety fence with a self-closing gate. Make sure that they are well maintained.
- Pool gate locks should be out of the reach of children and locked.
- Lock away all pool toys when not in use.
- Always keep pool chemicals locked away.
- Keep safety equipment by the pool. This includes a flotation device, a pole and /or a rope. Always bring a phone out to the pool.
- Use a pool motion detector that sets off an alarm should anyone fall in.
- Teach children to respect water when young.
- Enroll children early in drown proofing and swimming lessons.
- Keep furniture and yard equipment (ladders, wheelbarrows, etc. away from the pool fence.
- Keep the pool cover on when the pool is not in use. Keep water off the pool cover.
- Always keep the pool in good repair with all filter covers intact.
- Surround the pool with a non-slip surface.

The Bottom Line
Be A Great Parent

- Be an Aware and Prepared parent.
- Constantly be aware of potential dangers for your child.
- Danger-proof your home before your child is mobile.
- Be aware of your child's developmental stages and danger-proof according to the next anticipated stage.
- Know where your child is at all times.
  Adult supervision really means Adult Super Vision.
- Be prepared for accidents and illnesses.
- Learn infant CPR and stop-choking techniques before you deliver your baby.
- Learn basic first aid techniques.
- Have emergency phone numbers on or near the phone.
- Buy or make a first-aid kit and a first-medical kit.
- Learn to develop and trust your parents' intuition.
- Be a proactive parent.
- Educate yourself daily about baby concerns.
- Enjoy your baby, they grow up exceedingly fast.

Poison Control Agencies

UNITED STATES

ALABAMA
Alabama Poison Center --- Tuscaloosa
(800) 462-0800 (AL only); (205) 345-0600

Regional Poison Control Center
(205) 939-9201, (800) 292-6678 (AL only);
(205) 933-4050

ARIZONA
Arizona Poison and Drug Information Center
(800) 322-0101 (AZ only), (520) 626-6016

Good Samaritan Regional Medical Center
(800) 362-0101 (AZ only), (602) 253-3334

CALIFORNIA
California Poison Control System--Fresno
(800) 876-4766 (CA only)

California Poison Control System--San Diego
(800) 876-4766 (CA only)

California Poison Control System--Sacramento
(800) 876-4766 (CA only)

COLORADO
Rocky Mountain Poison and Drug Center
(800) 332-3073 (CO only) (303) 629-1123

CONNECTICUT
Connecticut Regional Poison Center
(800) 343-2722 (CT only)

DISTRICT OF COLUMBIA
National Capital Poison Center
(202) 625-3333; (202) 362-8563 (TTY)

FLORIDA
Florida Poison Information Center – Jacksonville
(904) 549-4480; (800) 282-3171 (FL only)

Florida Poison Information Center--Miami
(800) 282-3171 (FL only); (305) 585-5253

The Florida Poison Information Center
and Toxicology Resource Center
(813) 253-4444 (Tampa); (800) 282-3171 (FL)

GEORGIA
Georgia Poison Center
(800) 282-5846 (GA only); (404) 616-9000

INDIANA
Indiana Poison Center
800) 382-9097 (IN only), (317) 929-2323

KENTUCKY
Kentucky Regional Poison Center
(502) 589-8222

LOUISIANA
Louisiana Drug and Poison Information Center
(800) 256-9822 (LA only)

MARYLAND
Maryland Poison Center
(410) 528-7701, (800) 492-2414 (MD only)

National Capital Poison Center (D.C. suburbs)
(202) 625-3333; (202) 362-8563 (TTY)

MASSACHUSETTS
Massachusetts Poison Control
(617) 232-2120, (800) 682-9211 (MA only)

MICHIGAN
Blodgett Regional Poison Center
(800) 764-7661 (MI only)

Poison Control Center
(800) 764-7661 (MI only); (313) 745-5711

MINNESOTA
Hennepin Regional Poison Center
(612) 347-3141

Minnesota Regional Poison Center
(800) 222-1222 (MN only); (612) 221-2113

MISSOURI
Regional Poison Center
(314) 772-5200

MONTANA
Rocky Mountain Poison & Drug Center – Denver
(800) 525-5042 (MT only)

NEBRASKA
The Poison Center
(402) 354-5555 (Omaha), (800) 955-9119 (NE)

Poison Control Agencies
UNITED STATES

NEW JERSEY
New Jersey Poison Information and Education
(800) 764-7661 (NJ only)

NEW MEXICO
New Mexico Poison and Drug Information Center
(505) 843-2551, (800) 432-6866 (NM only)

NEW YORK
Central New York Poison Control Center
(315) 476-4766; (800) 252-5655 (NY only)

Finger Lakes Regional Poison Center
(800) 333-0542 (NY only), (716) 275-3232

Hudson Valley Regional Poison Center
(800) 336-6997 (NY only), (914) 366-3030

Long Island Regional Poison Control Center
(516) 542-2323

New York City Poison Control Center
(212) 340-4494, (212) P-O-I-S-O-N-S

NORTH CAROLINA
Carolinas Poison Center
(704) 355-4000, (800) 848-6946 (NC only)

OHIO
Central Ohio Poison Center
(614) 228-1323, (800) 682-7625 (OH only)

Cincinnati Drug & Poison Information Center and
Regional Poison Control System
(513) 558-5111, (800) 872-5111 (OH only)

OREGON
Oregon Poison Center
(503) 494-8968, (800) 452-7165 (OR only)

PENNSYLVANIA
Central Pennsylvania Poison Center
(800) 521-6110 (PA only)

The Poison Control Center
(800) 722-7112 (PA only); (215) 386-2100

Pittsburgh Poison Center
(412) 681-6669

RHODE ISLAND
Lifespan Poison Center
(401) 444-5727

TENNESSEE
Middle Tennessee Poison Center
(800) 288-9999 (TN only); (615) 936-2034

TEXAS
Central Texas Poison Center
(800) 764-7661 (TX only)

North Texas Poison Center
(800) 764-7661 (TX only)

Southeast Texas Poison Center
(409) 765-1420; (800) 764-7661(TX only)

West Texas Regional Poison Center
(800) 764-7661

UTAH
Utah Poison Control Center
(801) 581-2151, (800) 456-7707 (UT only)

VIRGINIA
Blue Ridge Poison Center
(804) 924-5543, (800) 451-1428 (VA only)

National Capital Poison Center (Northern VA)
(202) 625-3333

WASHINGTON
Washington Poison Center
(206) 526-2121; (800) 732-6985 (WA only)

WEST VIRGINIA
West Virginia Poison Center
(800) 642-3625 (WV only), (304) 348-4211

WYOMING
The Poison Center
(402) 390-5555 (Omaha), (800) 955-9119
(WY)

POISON CONTROL AGENCIES

Poison Control Agencies

CANADA

Children's Hospital of Eastern Ontario – Ottawa
Ontario Regional Poison Information Centre

(800) 267-1373 (Canada wide) or (613) 737-1100

ALBERTA
Poison and Drug Information Service
(800) 332-1414, (403) 670-1414

BRITISH COLUMBIA
Drug & Poison Information Centre --- Vancouver
(800) 567-8911, (604) 682-5050

MANITOBA
Provincial Poison Information Centre
(204) 787-2591

NEW BRUNSWICK
Poison Control Centre --- Moncton
(506) 857-5555
Emergency Department --- Saint John
(506) 648-6222

NEWFOUNDLAND & LABRADOR
Poison Control Centre --- St. John's
(709) 722-1110

NORTHWEST TERRITORIES
Poison Control Centre --- Yellowknife
(403) 669-4100

NOVA SCOTIA
Poison Control Centre --- Halifax
(800) 565-8161, (902) 428-8161 local

ONTARIO
Regional Poison Information Centre --- Ottawa
(800) 267-1373, (613) 737-1100 local

Regional Poison Information Centre --- Toronto
(800) 268-9017, (416) 598-5900 local

PRINCE EDWARD ISLAND
Poison Control Centre --- Halifax
(800) 565-8161

QUEBEC
Centre anti-poison du Québec --- Laval
(800) 463-5060, (418) 656-8090 local

SASKATCHEWAN
Poison Control Centre --- Regina
(800) 667-4545, (306) 766-4545 local

Poison Control Centre --- Saskatoon
(800) 363-7474, (306) 655-1010 local

YUKON TERRITORY
Poison Control Centre --- Whitehorse
(867) 667-8726

POISON CONTROL AGENCIES

Notes

Personal Information

Name: _____

Age: _____ Weight: _____

_____

Medication/Vitamins/Herbal Medicines: _____

_____

Allergies: _____

_____

Birth History: _____

_____

Medical History: _____

_____

_____

Surgical History: _____

_____

Family History of Significance: _____

_____

Immunization Record (including last Tetanus shot): __

_____

Parents should photocopy the following pages and fill in information for each child in the family. Parents should keep a copy of these forms in their wallet at all times and should bring these forms to all medical appointments.

Record of Illness

Name: _____

Date: _____ Time: _____

Temperature: _____ Time: _____

Temperature: _____ Time: _____

Other (changes in activity levels, appetite and attitude): _____

_____

_____

_____

Home Treatment (list all medications including herbal): _____

_____

_____

_____

Diagnoses: _____

_____

_____

Medical Treatment and Advice: _____

_____

_____

_____

_____

_____

Important Numbers

Emergency Services   **911**

Hospital

Police

Fire

Ambulance

Poison Control

Family Doctor

Pharmacy

Breastfeeding Health Professional

Important Numbers